ERP: The implementation cycle

ERP: The implementation cycle

Stephen Harwood

BUTTERWORTH
HEINEMANN

OXFORD AMSTERDAM BOSTON LONDON NEW YORK PARIS
SAN DIEGO SAN FRANCISCO SINGAPORE SYDNEY TOKYO

Butterworth-Heinemann
An imprint of Elsevier Science
Linacre House, Jordan Hill, Oxford OX2 8DP
200 Wheeler Road, Burlington, MA 01803

First published 2003

British Library Cataloguing in Publication Data
A catalogue record for this book is available from the British Library

ISBN 0 7506 52071

For information on all Butterworth-Heinemann publications visit
our website at www.bh.com

Composition by Genesis Typesetting Limited, Rochester, Kent
Printed and bound in Great Britain by MPG Books Ltd, Bodmin

Contents

Contents

Contents

Computer Weekly Professional Series

There are few professions which require as much continuous updating as that of the IS executive. Not only does the hardware and software scene change relentlessly, but also ideas about the actual management of the IS function are being continuously modified, updated and changed. Thus keeping abreast of what is going on is really a major task.

The Butterworth-Heinemann – *Computer Weekly* Professional Series has been created to assist IS executives keep up to date with the management ideas and issues of which they need to be aware.

One of the key objectives of the series is to reduce the time it takes for leading edge management ideas to move from the academic and consulting environments into the hands of the IT practitioner. Thus this series employs appropriate technology to speed up the publishing process. Where appropriate some books are supported by CD ROM or by additional information or templates located on the Web.

This series provides IT professionals with an opportunity to build up a bookcase of easily accessible, but detailed information on the important issues that they need to be aware of to successfully perform their jobs.

Aspiring or already established authors are invited to get in touch with me directly if they would like to be published in this series.

Dr Dan Remenyi
Series Editor
Dan.remenyi@mcil.co.uk

Series Editor
Dan Remenyi, Visiting Professor, Trinity College Dublin

Advisory Board
Frank Bannister, Trinity College Dublin
Ross Bentley, Management Editor, *Computer Weekly*
Egon Berghout, Technical University of Delft, The Netherlands
Ann Brown, City University Business School, London
Roger Clark, The Australian National University
Reet Cronk, Harding University, Arkansas, USA
Arthur Money, Henley Management College, UK
Sue Nugus, MCIL, UK
Rene Pellissier, School of Business Leadership, Johannesburg
David Taylor, CERTUS, UK
Terry White, BentleyWest, Johannesburg

Other titles in the Series
Considering computer contracting?
Corporate politics for IT managers: how to get streetwise
David Taylor's Inside Track
Delivering IT and e-business value
e-Business implementation
e-Business strategies for virtual organizations
The effective measurement and management of IT costs and benefits
A hacker's guide to project management
How to become a successful IT consultant
How to manage the IT helpdesk (2nd edition)
Information warfare: corporate attack and defence in a digital world
IT investment – making a business case
Knowledge management – a blueprint for delivery
Make or break issues in IT management
Making IT count
Network security
Prince 2: a practical handbook
The project manager's toolkit
Reinventing the IT department
Stop IT project failures through risk management
Subnet design for efficient networks
Understanding the Internet

x

Preface

This book was written following over fifteen years of work in both academic and industrial situations in the area of Enterprise Information Management Systems and process re-engineering. This culminated in the implementation of several Information Systems within small and medium-sized companies. What was apparent was the profusion of potential problems that lay before me. Articles in the press, trade press and on the Internet provided superficial glimpses into these problems. However, there was no coherent total picture of how these problems related to each other. Furthermore, even the best of companies appear to suffer from these problems. As such, it was difficult to know how best to plan and proceed with an implementation.

This book attempts to provide the reader with the layout of an implementation. The aim is to provide a picture of what is involved in an implementation, starting from the realization that there is a need to embark on this course of action. Whilst the focus is upon a single-site, single-business operation, many of the issues are relevant to multisite/multibusiness operations. A simple approach is adopted, based on a variety of personal experiences.

It is envisaged that this book will appeal to those who are new to ERP, yet who have a need to understand what is involved in the implementation of an ERP system. This may be an owner or manager of a small or medium-sized business or a newly appointed project manager of a larger organization.

This account reveals the scale and scope of an implementation, what to prepare for, what questions to ask of the vendor during the selection and questions to ask of the selected vendor's consultants assisting with implementation. It alerts the reader to the dilemma that both technologies and vendors change rapidly. It allows the reader to anticipate potential problems and hopefully avoid them. Areas, covered elsewhere in greater detail, are dealt with here more in an introductory manner. A selected reading list will help direct the reader to relevant sources. With regard to the handling of the multitude of technological issues, these are not dealt with in any depth.

Where technical issues are introduced, this is in order to make the reader aware of them.

It should be noted that not all problems are identified. Every situation is different and there will always be something that will be particular to each organization. Nevertheless, the material presented should be sufficient to alert the reader to the warning signs of a potential problem. It is up to the reader to take the appropriate action.

Good luck.

Stephen Harwood

Acknowledgements

To write this book without assistance would have been difficult if not impossible. Much of the material draws upon my years in research and as a practitioner within the information management domain. During this time, I have had contact with many people who have helped shape my ideas. To name them would be impossible, but to those unnamed persons, I thank you for our discussions.

However, whilst writing this book a number of individuals have played a particular role in helping me. Paul Watts of Benchmark Research Ltd contributed market research information. Daniel Miklovic and Howard Dresner of Gartner Inc. made respective contributions about aspects of the ERP sector. Dr David Wainwright, Reader in Information Systems at the School of Informatics, Northumbria University, provided invaluable comments about the implementation issues. Elaine, my partner, gave her undivided support.

To them I express my deepest thanks, thanks and more thanks.

About the author

Stephen Harwood has worked with IT since reading the subject as part of his first degree in the late 1970s. His first hand experience of ERP is underpinned by over 15 years' activity in the fields of information management, organizational change and business strategy. During this time he has gained experience of many aspects of a business's activities. Roles have included researcher, facilitator, manager and director. His particular interest is the role of Information and Communication Technologies as an enabler of strategic intent. He is currently working in a freelance capacity.

Introduction

ERP is the acronym for Enterprise Resource Planning. ERP has its roots in manufacturing, although it has evolved in a remarkably short time to address many other functions and sectors. The implementation of an ERP application is about organizational change. The focus of the ERP implementation is the ERP system. The ERP system can simply be described as an integrated information system servicing all aspects of the business. It handles transactions, maintains records, provides real time information and facilitates planning and control. However, its effectiveness is an outcome of the success of the implementation life cycle.

An ERP implementation should not be viewed purely as an IT project. It is a multidisciplinary team effort. It cuts into the very heart of the business, upturning policies, practices and power-bases. It is indiscriminate in who it stresses and strains. It requires a changing set of skills, which may at times be unique to the moment, never to be used again. If it is successful then the rewards are bountiful. Transactions are speedily processed. Timely information provides awareness of what is happening. Actions become more proactive. The payback has a positive effect on the bottom line.

However, it is easy for an ERP implementation to go wrong. Furthermore, it can be difficult to put things right. The further into the implementation life cycle, the harder it can become to put things right and the greater the associated cost. Despite all the research and experience available, it may come as a surprise that implementations can, and do, go wrong, leading in some cases to high-profile legal battles.

1.1 Using this book

The aim of this book is to guide the reader around the myriad of different issues affecting an ERP implementation. To achieve this, a simple model of an implementation has been developed. This model views an ERP implementation as a cycle of events. This cycle is presented in Figure 1.1.

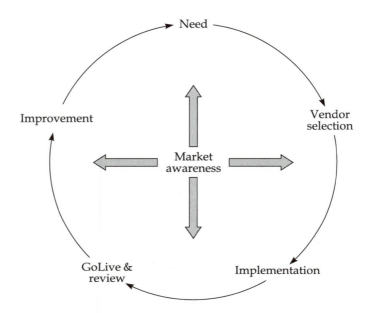

Figure 1.1
The ERP
implementation cycle

The implementation life cycle starts at the point when the **need** is recognized for a new information system. The existing system is inadequate and there is a need to do something. **Market awareness** provides an appreciation of the technology available and those providing it. This leads to the **vendor selection** process whereby a solution is sought to meet this need. The **implementation** of the solution is a complex event involving many people and culminates in the transition to a **GoLive** state. The adoption of a continuous **improvement** programme after the GoLive period enables the benefits of the system to be fully exploited. Eventually the cycle concludes with the recognition that the replacement system is inadequate and that the **need** arises again to do something. Within this cycle are a host of different activities. A breakdown of this cycle into its main activities is presented in Table 1.1.

The story begins with an attempt to develop an **awareness** of what is going on in the marketplace. Whilst relevant at all stages

Table 1.1 A breakdown of the ERP implementation cycle

Stage	Focus	Activity	Chapters/ Section(s)
0 Market awareness	Marketplace	Understand what is going on in the marketplace	2, 3, 4, 5
1 Define need	Requirements	Establish why	6.1
	Cost-benefits	Establish costs and determine benefits	6.2, 6.3
	Requirements	Determine requirements	7
2 Select vendor	Vendor offerings and fit	Establish selection process	8.1
		Execute selection process	8.2
		'Close the deal'	9
3 Implement project	Create and maintain conditions for project implementation	Establish and assign project participant roles	11.2.1
		Establish, monitor and maintain commitment	11.2.1
		Define scope	11.2.2
		Produce, monitor and update plan	11.2.3
		Establish, monitor and update budget	11.2.4
		Set up and manage problem resolution mechanisms	11.2.5
		Assess and contain risks	11.2.6
		Establish, monitor and manage performance	11.2.7
		Manage vendor relationships	11.2.8
		Install and commission hardware, software and networks	11.3
		Develop training strategy	11.4
	Implement project plan	Train project team	12.1
		Define and develop processes	12.2, 12.3
		Modify software	12.3.2
		Test (pilot) processes	12.4
		Establish and assign responsibilities for processes	12.5
		Design and create documentation	12.6
		Train users	12.7
		Set up data	12.8
	GoLive	Resolve problems	13.1
		Review	13.2
4 Post-GoLive improvements	Process performance	Improve processes	14

of the ERP life cycle, the level of awareness varies according to the necessity to participate in this marketplace. Obviously the most critical stage is when going through the process of vendor selection. However, the marketplace should not be neglected during the other stages. When alerted to the possible need for a new system the marketplace can provide a reference with which to confirm this need. During the implementation and post-GoLive review, there may be little interest as attention focuses upon the bought system. Nevertheless, it is not unknown for a vendor's offering to be abandoned in favour of another if problems become insurmountable. Later, during the improvement stage, interest lies with improving practices and getting more out of the functionality, looking at specialist packages to boost functionality if necessary. Finally, there comes a point in time when the implementation has completed its cycle: there is a need to do something, either upgrade or move to another package and again attention focuses upon what is going on in the marketplace.

The first three chapters are concerned primarily with the technology. The development of ERP is reviewed from its earliest beginnings (Chapter 2). By understanding how the technology has evolved, it becomes possible to develop a better appreciation of what is available (Chapter 3), where it is heading and what to watch out for (Chapter 4). This alerts us as to what is or might become redundant. This also allows us to distinguish between sales hype and what is actually available. With the technology becoming so intricate and prone to rapid change it is easy to lose perspective.

Chapter 5 focuses on developments in the marketplace. This is also an ever-changing landscape which will surprise the unaware. Established names do disappear. There is always the danger of a purchased application becoming unsupported if a company collapses or is acquired by another. A five-year investment in an ERP application is a long time during which much can happen.

The next two chapters are about issues relating to the **need** for an ERP application. Chapter 6 is divided into three sections. The first explores possibilities about why is there a need. The second section raises at an early stage the issue of cost. Whilst details about costs may not emerge until later in the implementation cycle, an appreciation of likely costs and their breakdown is required up-front to facilitate planning and guide negotiations. Likewise, the third section, which is about the possible benefits, provides an opportunity to assess the value of the proposed project. Chapter 7 addresses the question of what the requirements are and how these requirements are to be provided. Part of this process involves defining requirements. Whilst there are different approaches to this, the reader is referred to Section 12.2, which provides both a theoretical framework for understanding what a process is and a method for collecting the required data.

Chapters 8 and 9 explore issues relating to the **vendor selection** process. A method is presented which enables detailed profiles of vendors and their offerings to be generated. The aim is to get a good fit between requirements and offerings. This is also the opportunity to establish whether it is possible to develop a good working relationship with the vendor. Once contracts have been exchanged it becomes increasingly difficult to break the relationship off.

The **project implementation** stage of the selected ERP application is the part of the implementation life cycle that many people focus on when thinking about an ERP implementation. This is where the main costs are incurred and where problems are most likely to manifest. An introduction to the problems that tend to be associated with an implementation is presented in Chapter 10. The next two chapters explore issues in relation to what can be described as the preparation (Chapter 11) and execution (Chapter 12) phases of the project. The preparation involves the creation and maintenance of the conditions for the successful execution of the project. The execution itself involves a series of activities focused upon business processes. These include process design, development and testing, training of users and the production of support materials. Section 12.2.1 deviates from all the other sections in that it presents a theoretical framework with which to understand what a process is. The intention is that by having a deeper understanding, then issues relating to processes can be more effectively recognized and acted upon.

Chapter 13 deals with the issues relating to **GoLive**. The number of problems that emerge at this stage are a reflection of the rigour of the process design and development activities. Do the processes do what is required of them?

The process of **improvement** which should kick in at some point in time after the GoLive, when processes have had time to settle down, is explored in Chapter 14. It is during this phase that many of the benefits can be realized. However, a point is reached when the system is viewed more as a hindrance than as an enabler. It is then that the cycle is closed and questions are asked about whether to upgrade the system or seek out a new package (Section 14.2).

The book closes by briefly reflecting upon key issues (Chapter 15). Although this book attempts to provide insight into the issues relating to the ERP implementation life cycle, the reality of an implementation is characterized by its complexity. Furthermore, things do not always work out as expected, despite all the preparation and good intentions. Nevertheless, for those that complete the course, the effort is often deemed worthwhile.

Additional material is provided for the reader. A Selected reading list presents the details of books which complement the material presented here. It is neither an exhaustive list nor a 'best of' list. Rather, it presents titles that I have found useful. Likewise, a list of Useful sources is presented which identifies a selection of websites that the reader may find useful. The last section is the ubiquitous list of Acronyms and abbreviations, and their expanded versions.

2

Historical perspective

The story begins in the early 1960s when the commercial availability of computers provided a breakthrough in data processing capability. This was readily exploited through the development of inventory management systems for manufacturing. The first of these was the BOMP (Bill of Material Processor). From this, software was developed that enabled future material requirements to be determined; in other words, these were material ordering and planning systems. These Material Requirements Planning (MRP) systems tended to be written by the organizations using them and were mainframe based. It was during the 1960s that IBM developed its own concept of an integrated production and inventory management system. This reflected the realization that the production schedule drove material requirements. This concept was published in early 1972 as the COPICS (Communications Orientated Production Information and Control System) 'black books'. Its importance lay in the fact that it detailed the data flow structure for a manufacturing system. Nevertheless, by this time MRP systems were established in a limited number of US companies. In 1971, the 'MRP crusade' took off, sponsored by APICS (American Production and Inventory Control Society). This led to a rapid rise in the number of implementations during the 1970s. MRP developed to incorporate Capacity Requirements Planning (CRP) and Sales and Operations Planning (SOP). Thus, 'closed loop' MRP emerged. In 1975, the concepts for MRP were published in the seminal work of Joseph Orlicky.[1] MRP was quickly becoming a widely accepted and used production tool.

The next major step was at the start of the 1980s. Instead of being confined to the planning and control of materials, the scope of the system broadened to incorporate all manufacturing resources. Furthermore, it could be integrated with the finance function. This improved awareness of the cost implications of operational activities. Oliver Wight termed this Manufacturing Resource Planning (MRPII), emphasizing that the application was manufacturing.[2] The decreasing cost/increasing performance of computing together with the increasing availability of software applications fuelled the growth in the number of systems implemented. However, the applications often needed modification, since, usually, only the basic functionality was catered for. Functionality became more sophisticated when modifications were rolled out as standard features in later versions. The extent of this functionality is illustrated in the architecture diagram of Figure 2.1. However, it was being realized that many implementations failed to meet expectations. This led to attempts to understand the problems associated with implementations. Nevertheless MRPII established itself in many manufacturing companies amongst the growing list of complementary technologies, e.g. JIT, OPT, TQM. (The papers by

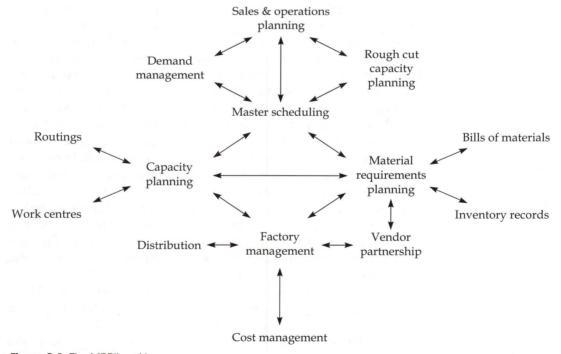

Figure 2.1 The MRPII architecture

Don Ralston[3] and Randall Sadowski[4] provide more detailed accounts of the emergence of MRPII.)

The 1980s were also a period for the development of the concept of CIM (Computer Integrated Manufacturing). Underlying this was the philosophy of the fully automated and integrated factory. Hardware and software developments enabled integration between product design (Computer Aided Design, CAD) and manufacturing equipment (Computer Aided Manufacturing, CAM). However, this application captured only one aspect of the dimensions of CIM. Boaden and Dale (1986)[5] identified ten ways of perceiving CIM. These ranged from single issue definitions (e.g. CAD/CAM) through information systems definitions (e.g. MRPII) to very broad, all encompassing definitions (e.g. the total organization). Underpinning all was the concept of integration.

This integration was facilitated by the widespread need to develop and implement standards that enabled technologies to interface. In 1978, the International Standards Organisation published the Open Standards Interconnection (OSI) Reference Model. It provided the framework for developing standards for all data communications. General Motors, who had many thousands of isolated units of technology, by the end of the 1970s faced the difficulty of technology incompatibility and the high cost of making them communicate. Boeing faced similar issues. Based on the OSI framework, by 1985, they had respectively published Manufacturing Automation Protocol (MAP) and Technical and Office Protocols. Since then, many developments have emerged (e.g. Ethernet, Token Ring, SNA, TCP/IP) that allow technologies to interface seamlessly.

Another 1980s development was the technology to capture, store, retrieve, distribute and process documents/images, in other words, image/document management systems. From this emerged what has become known as workflow. By the early 1990s, the concept of workflow had expanded beyond the processing of document/images to broadly encompass the automation of processes. Workflow was defined as 'concerned with the automation of procedures where documents, information or tasks are passed between participants according to a defined set of rules to achieve, or contribute to, an overall business goal' (Workflow Management Coalition).[6] Dedicated commercial workflow packages became available which allowed stable, high volume, routine task sequences to be technology driven and controlled. It was a costly solution, which restricted its adoption to mainly larger organizations. During the 1990s, workflow technology increasingly became a feature of ERP applications and more recently as an integral feature of CRM applications, e.g. call centre processes.

The 1990s saw the rise of powerful PCs, client-servers and both local-area networks (LANs) and wide-area networks (WANs). The first microprocessors were released in 1971. Moore's law states that the number of transistors on a chip will double every two years. This doubling of performance every few years, coupled with the continual reduction in the cost of a chip, had, by the 1990s, led to the widespread availability of relatively cheap, powerful computing facilities.

Another innovation that affected user uptake was the development of a user-friendly alternative to the ubiquitous and uninviting text screen interface. The Graphical User Interface (GUI) was a late-1970s innovation that was adopted and commercially exploited by Apple during the 1980s. The commercial breakthrough for DOS based PCs came with Microsoft's release of Windows 3.0 in May 1990. The GUI has made it far easier for people to adapt to computer technology and to use increasingly complex applications.

The development of national network spines together with the expansion and interconnectivity of other networks resulted in the Internet bursting out upon the world during the mid-1990s (Section 2.3). This, in turn, triggered the explosive growth in the use of e-mail. E-mail had been in use since the 1960s but was restricted to what were numerous isolated small groups of interconnected users, found within mainframe or early-networked environments. In 1981, Haynes launched the first commercial modem. During the 1980s a number of commercial organizations emerged, including Compu-Serv and America Online. They provided modem based dial-in subscription services, which included e-mail. This was the dawn of home-user networking which was to be followed by the Internet.

In 1990, Gartner Inc., a US company providing advice about business technology, had introduced the acronym 'ERP' (Enterprise Resource Planning).

A concept developed by Gartner Group describing the next generation of manufacturing business systems and manufacturing resource planning (MRPII) software. It includes the client/server architecture, uses graphical user interfaces (GUIs) and can be crafted with open systems. Beyond the standard functionality that is offered, other features are included (e.g. quality, process operations management and regulatory reporting). In addition, the base technology used in ERP will give users software and hardware independence as well as an easy upgrade path. Key to ERP is the way in which users can tailor the application so it is intrinsically easy to use (Gartner Inc. definition: www.gartner.com).

The main distinctions between MRPII and ERP are arguably technology focused rather than concerned with significant changes in functionality. The main innovation appears to have been the shift to a client-server architecture.

From a functionality perspective there were a number of innovations that emerged during the 1990s. First, there was the development of specialist packages targeted at meeting clearly defined functional requirements. These included Supply Chain Planning (SCP), Product Data Management (PDM) and Customer Relationship Management (CRM). At the same time, there was the emergence of non-manufacturing applications for use in such areas as the service industries, e.g. asset management and field service support. The latter half of the 1990s saw e-commerce fervour, culminating in vendor's rhetoric about their e-enabled offerings. This was aside from the independent software developments that had been taking place over time in such sectors as banking, insurance and retail.

Supply Chain Planning (SCP), discussed further in Section 2.4, is aimed at providing a better fit between customer demand, production schedules and material delivery, resulting in reduced inventory and better resource utilization. Under the umbrella of Supply Chain Management, associated functionality includes warehouse management, transportation and procurement.

Product Data Management (PDM) provides support to the engineering design process. It derives its initial source data directly from the CAD. It controls design changes and their approval, all associated documentation, including supplier data sheets downloaded via the Internet, and provides a full history of the design development.

Customer Relationship Management (CRM), discussed further in Section 2.5, is concerned with the customer facing front-end business activities, e.g. sales, field service, call centre and marketing.

With the development of specialist 'best-of-breed' packages and the increasing tendency for partnership relationships between these providers and the ERP vendors the issue of integration became even more important. It saw the shift away from individual and expensive interface programming to the adoption of interface standards enabling use of middleware packages such as ODBC. One new specification for Internet interconnectivity, developed by IBM and Microsoft, is Universal, Description, Discovery and Integration (UDDI).

By the turn of the millennium, the emerging range of Enterprise Application Software, dominated by ERP, had evolved into an uncompromisingly complex compilation of modules and not so integrated applications.

The following sections take a more detailed look at five of the main developments. Section 2.1 focuses upon the desire to maximize the opportunity for getting useful information from the data. Information systems have, over time, developed a notorious reputation for withholding information. Various attempts to overcome this have resulted in the emergence of various tools (Executive Information Systems (EIS), Business Intelligence (BI)), which make it increasingly easier to obtain the information sought.

The remaining four sections (2.2–2.5) examine specific developments relating to a business's interface. The first of these, EDI, could be described as the precursor to the second, e-commerce. Whilst some might argue that EDI has been superseded by e-commerce, there is an argument that EDI is experiencing a revival as a result of technological developments associated with e-commerce and is now an enabling technology under the e-commerce umbrella. Much hyped e-commerce exploits Internet and World Wide Web technologies to provide a complementary channel in support of business related interactions. The third and fourth developments, SCP and CRM, are more specifically focused on suppliers and customers respectively, enabled by developments in both information and communication technologies.

2.1 Executive Information Systems (EIS), Business Intelligence (BI) and data value

It has long since been recognized that the data captured on computing systems offers a source of information. However, the question that is often asked is: How? Whilst standard reports are ideal for routine standard enquiries, they are inadequate for ad hoc enquiries and do not volunteer anything anomalous or interesting that is happening. Useful information has been, for a long time, lost within the database. Nevertheless, there have been various developments aimed at exploiting the potential of data.

During the 1970s, Decision Support Systems (DSS) became available. These enabled the analysis of large volumes of data. However it can be argued that they failed as decision support tools since the nature of the information provided was contrary to the ad hoc nature of an executive's information requirements and the informal methods used by executives when seeking out information.

The 1980s saw the emergence of Executive Information Systems (EIS). These attempted to provide top-level views of the business focusing on key performance measures. They were user friendly and offered exception reporting and trend analysis. Data was often presented in a graphical form. When a deviation from the norm occurred an alert would be triggered. This deviation could then be drilled down to the raw data and the detail examined. Leading providers were MetaPraxis (established in 1984) with 'Resolve', Comshare with 'Commander' (which evolved from a late 1960s DSS), marketed in the UK by Thorn EMI, and Pilot Executive Software (US) with 'Pilot' (launched in 1984). In general, EISs had limited success.

In 1993, Dr Codd created the term 'OnLine Analytical Processing'[7] (OLAP). This relates to the means for analysing data based upon his research into relational databases. It encompasses the set of tools used for the 'collection, management, processing and presenting of data for analysis purposes'.[8] Strictly speaking, for a product to be an OLAP tool it must adhere to Codd's twelve rules, though observance to this code appears to be lax. These rules include having multidimensional data manipulation, a client-server architecture, flexible reporting and multiuser support. The first desktop product was 'PowerPlay', released in 1990 by COGNOS. Since then a number of products have been launched. Usage commonly includes sales analysis.

Two other dominant concepts emerged during the mid-1990s: Data Warehousing and Data Mining. The former relates to the link up and analysis of multiple databases. Deceptively simple, this is a minefield for the database illiterate. The complexity arises in the database structures and their linkage. Data Mining is concerned with the searching out of relationships, patterns and trends hidden in the data, using powerful statistical engines.

In 1989, Gartner Inc. began using the term 'Business Intelligence' (BI). The aim was to:

establish and popularise BI, as an umbrella concept, to describe the ways in which end users get value from quantitative information. After some early excitement between 1992 and 1995, 'Business Intelligence' fell into disuse. Many vendors were seeking something new and fresh. 'Data discovery', 'data mining', 'information access', 'data insight', 'business insight' and others started to emerge.[9]

However, by 1998, the term Business Intelligence had taken hold.

Business Intelligence, as envisaged by Gartner Inc. in 1989, entails the use of the aforementioned technologies that emerged during the 1990s to interrogate data. These technologies have resulted in powerful new ways of getting value out of the data. Their set up does require technical expertise and they can be viewed as expensive. Nevertheless, they offer advantages of enabling interactive analysis by users who have only limited technical knowledge about the tools; the data is presented in a user friendly and visually agreeable manner; the analysis is real-time, overcoming the delays inherent in earlier tools; furthermore, the analysis can be easily distributed to others. The products have tended to be developed by niche vendors rather than by ERP developers. However, it is not uncommon for partnership agreements to be in-place so that compatible Business Intelligence tools can seamlessly bolt onto the ERP offering. The important point is that these tools can only generate value if they can access the relevant data. The client needs to be aware of data access limitations of the ERP system, because some of the potentially required data fields may be inaccessible. Perhaps more importantly, the data must be error free.

2.2 Electronic Data Interchange (EDI)

The UK's National Economic Development Council has defined EDI as:

the transfer of structured data, by agreed message standards, from one computer system to another, by electronic means.[10]

EDI was developed in the USA during the 1970s as a means for transmitting routine transaction related messages between businesses. Its uptake was slow, with the perceived benefits of automated business-to-business transactions being offset by:

- the number of standards and their variants that companies could adopt; three standards dominated: ANSI X12 (US), EDIFACT (Europe), TRADACOMS (UK), and
- the time required for its development.

A company might find itself dealing with a number of companies each using a different standard or a different variant of a standard. Furthermore, each transaction type required an inordinate amount of work for both parties involved in the transaction. Companies also had reservations about information being lifted from and downloaded onto their information systems. Their distrust revolved around the idea of someone being able to place data on their systems without it being checked! However, its attraction was that it was a secure and reliable means for automating frequent standard commercial transactions between the information systems of trading businesses. The cost efficiencies would be gained from the volume of transactions handled, which would otherwise be carried out manually with the risk of data entry error. Uptake was mainly by the larger companies.

The basic principle was that a message would have a clearly defined format. The required data would be uploaded from the company's database, translated into an ASCII file and then converted into an EDI standard format suitable for transmission. It was transmitted over a secure, dedicated network provided by a Value Added Network provider (e.g. Geis, BT, AT&T). The message was received, translated back into an ASCII file and then into an appropriate format for either downloading into the recipient's database or for printing out if there was reluctance to interface into the database. Since it was an electronic transaction, the terms and conditions relating to this transaction were subject to prior agreement.

With the emergence of the Internet, it was realized that this could offer an alternative channel to that offered by the Value Added Network (VAN) providers. The attraction of VAN providers was that they provided back-up, security and enabled interconnectivity with other VANs. However, transmissions were costly, which was another uptake deterrent to smaller businesses. The Internet-EDI technology uses the traditional EDI message, but encrypts it before it is transmitted over public networks, either using e-mail or by FTP file transfer. The one pitfall is the need for the same technology at either end of the transmission line, though this may cost far less than the cost associated with traditional EDI. The Internet offers real-time transmission compared to the slower traditional EDI. It also opens up the number of trading partners since the development costs and time are significantly reduced. However, whether encryption is viewed as secure is open to debate.

Internet-EDI technology is still under development and its future role is unclear. Security concerns, whether real or imaginary, need to be overcome. Alternatives to EDI, such as web portals, may emerge and displace EDI from its long-established position. Whatever the future, it now appears that EDI is viewed as a subset of e-commerce.

2.3 Emergence of e-commerce

The innovation that has opened up new worlds to people has its roots in the 1960s.[11] Research took place into how computers could communicate with each other. The result was the development of one of the first computer networks, ARPANET, linking a number of US universities. During the 1970s, ARPANET grew as more universities connected to the network. As the technology evolved, a standard emerged, Transmission Control Protocol/Internet Protocol (TCP/IP). This enabled different technologies to be connected together and hence facilitated the connection of other networks. Whilst the early networks served, primarily, the academic community and US Government departments, their commercial potential was recognized. Private organizations linked their networks into the establishing infrastructure. During the 1980s, the number of connected computers rose from under 1000 to over 100 000.[12] Initial uses included electronic mail, file-sharing and remote access. By 1992, the number of connected computers had broken through one million, exploding to five million in 1995 and 100 million in 2000.

One of the main contributions to the explosive adoption of the Internet in the 1990s was the invention of the World Wide Web (WWW). In 1989, Tim Berners-Lee, based at CERN, put forward a proposal for a hypertext-based information retrieval system (WWW) using a browser interface. The purpose was to improve access to information. Starting work on it the following year, he developed it into a functioning system. In 1992, CERN released the browser as freeware. The concept of a browser attracted other people and other browsers were developed, of which

Netscape, formed in 1994, became a leading provider. The ease of browser adoption and use led to an explosion in the number of people accessing what was referred to as the World Wide Web (the name originally given to Tim Berners-Lee's project). In addition to e-mail, these people could access a wide range of informative sites and download files.

One supposition that emerged was that this captured pool of on-line people provided a potential pool of customers. This led to the development of on-line facilities to enable these 'customers' to search catalogues, select and purchase both products and services and then pay for them using a credit card This was despite security concerns about the potential for fraud, which was later to be very much founded. Nevertheless, the attraction of easy access to customers spawned the vision of a new type of business dealing with customers (B2C) through the Internet. The few years between 1996 and 1998 led to intense venture investment and a boom in the setting up of dot com businesses. Although a number of millionaires were made, the boom did not last. Several factors led to this collapse. These businesses had over-expectations about potential customer demand and thus were unable to attain a sufficient turnover to cover costs. Furthermore, many of these businesses failed to develop a solid infrastructure to meet demand and thus were unable to follow through on a transaction. In 2000, both investor confidence and a significant number of these virtual businesses collapsed, including the high profile Boo.com. The delusion of easy money was to be replaced by the return of business prudence.

However, at the same time as the B2C developments it was also appreciated that there was a tremendous opportunity for businesses to deal with each other through this new medium (B2B). Many of these interested companies were established brick and mortar companies. Their web presence appeared to follow a pattern. The initial offering was an Internet web-presence that provided visitors with information about their activities. The next development was facilities that people could use through their browsers, e.g. purchase ordering. Different classes of users were distinguishable which included internal company employees, business customers, subscription users and the general public. Intranets were developed, which limited access to those within the company, and also extranets, which allowed authorized access by external people. This led to the development of web-capability for ERP, SCM and CRM applications.

The concepts of e-procurement and e-commerce in the business context have extended beyond the Intranet and the WWW to incorporate interactions in what can be called e-space. These incorporate any mode of electronic interaction between customers and suppliers including EDI (Section 2.2), e-mail and video-conferencing. The effect has been to change, and in some cases revolutionize, the way companies interact with each other. In addition to direct contact with each other, the concept of the electronic marketplace ('virtual' trading exchanges or e-marketplaces) has arisen. Although not new (electronic trading was introduced into the London Stock Exchange in 1986), it offers an alternative to direct contact. It provides a virtual environment where buyers and sellers can meet and trade for a small commission. Nevertheless, despite the plethora of exchanges set up, whether many of them receive a viable level of business remains to be seen. As with B2C, the uptake of B2B dealings has been well below expectations though in this case, business exposure to this appears to be a lot less.

Irrespective of whether the application is B2C, B2B or e-marketplace, the opportunities for commercial e-space interactions are relatively undeveloped with many, sometimes expensive, mistakes having been made. It can be easily forgotten that the technologies only found their way into the public domain in the mid-1990s. E-procurement and e-commerce has widely been described as a new philosophy and a way of doing business with a new set of business rules. However, perhaps this is an illusion!

Whilst the Internet and WWW have opened up a very powerful and not to be underestimated channel between customer and suppliers, the new set of practices that have resulted should not be mistaken for a new set of rules about how business should be conducted. The rules have not changed. The business must be founded upon a sound strategy, financial control, and operational and logistical efficiencies. Profit and loss, cash flow and balance sheet remain key measures. The relatively few successful dot coms, e.g. Amazon and Yahoo, appear to have recognized this. The successful companies operating in e-space, whether B2C or B2B, have tended to be traditional brick and mortar companies that have a solid infrastructure in place to support the exploitation of the opportunities of this new channel. They have recognized that this new channel may require new and perhaps radically different practices, e.g. consider the explosion in the number of call centres. They also recognize that it is a complementary channel not a replacement channel nor the sole channel for the business.

Underpinning the development of this new channel is an understanding of the processes involved. Although words relating to these processes may be prefixed with 'e-', they are no different from any other processes in terms of the principles underpinning their understanding, design and implementation. However, this channel has several characteristics that need to be recognized. These are speed, reach and visibility. Interactions are faster via the Internet than by traditional means. Responses need to be appropriate and timely. The Internet is open globally to anyone with access to it. A sudden surge in people wishing access to the site can bring its collapse, e.g. the English 1901 Census website. Inefficiencies associated with any dealings using the Internet are more readily exposed. When problems are experienced, this creates a bad impression and deters the return of visitors. This places great pressure on getting the processes and the technology supporting e-commerce right.

However, there is another dimension that is raising its profile. This dimension is less concerned about the performance of the e-commerce channels and concerned more about matters relating to the conduct associated with use of the Internet and e-commerce. An interesting article in *Computer Weekly*[13] high-lights four headings relating to conduct: security, legal, intellectual property and privacy. Concerns about security issues have already been mentioned. From a legal perspective, issues range from international harmonization of laws and national juris-diction to false representation and fraudulent trading. The Intellectual Property debate has dwelled on the ownership of domain names but it is also concerned about the content of websites and the enforcement of copyright laws. Privacy includes such issues as the placing of cookies on user systems, the use and passing on of personal details collected through websites and the practice of spamming (the sending of unwant-ed e-mail). Progress on the conduct dimension appears to be slow and undermines confidence in e-commerce. Time will tell how this arena will develop.

2.4 Supply Chain Planning (SCP)

MRP grew out of the need to know what to buy and when it was to be delivered. However, this is subject to many variables, starting with the customer. What does the customer want and when? Furthermore, customers are known to be fickle, change their minds and cancel the order or order something different. If several customers behave like this then trying to match material purchases with production geared to meet customer delivery dates becomes a juggling nightmare. Variables to consider include production capacity, machine availability, supplier and production lead-times, product Bills of Materials, available raw material stock and available finished product stock. The goal was always to minimize the level of inventory held yet still meet customer demand. MRP, MRPII and ERP provided only limited solutions.

In recognition of the problems of balancing supply with demand various practices emerged during the 1980s. Sales and Operations Planning provided a high level overview of the match between supply and demand. Just-In-Time (JIT) deliveries were based on a card/bin system. This indicated which items were required and triggered the 'call-off' of these items from the supplier, who held an agreement to have a stock of these items available for requirements. Product development adopted the idea of collaboration between customer and supplier at the design stage. Expertise shared at this stage enabled the design out of costs and the development of standardized parts in order to reduce the size of the component pool and to gain economies of scale when sourcing.

The fundamental task of dealing with the complexity of planning created an opportunity for vendors (e.g. i2, Manugistics and Preactor) to develop specialist planning products. These integrate customer forecasts and demand with operational constraints, including capacity and availability, to generate production schedules and purchasing requirements. These powerful modelling tools are presented under the banners of 'Supply Chain Planning' (SCP) and 'Advanced Planning Systems' (APS). Whether there is any distinction between the two is open to debate. Despite all this sophistication, these planning tools are exposed to weaknesses in forecasts. An optimistic or pessimistic forecast passed from a retailer to its distributor will be magnified as it is transmitted back up the supply chain and could have an undesirable effect upon inventory and availability.

Other functional developments have emerged. Maintenance, Repair and Overhaul (MRO) can deal with the large number of part numbers, small quantities of each part and a myriad of suppliers associated with equipment maintenance. Different inventory requirements can be managed, whether these are in hubs, multisite warehouses or different inventory accounts within one location. Replenishment systems can also be handled. Transport management includes transportation scheduling and real-time monitoring and the tracking of items and/or vehicles in-transit. The Internet has fuelled the development of self-service malls and on-line auctions where buyers and sellers can engage in trade.

Collectively, the suite of functionality on offer provides fairly comprehensive supply chain focused support to the practices associated with the concept of Supply Chain Management (SCM). However, one should beware of the interchangeable use of SCP and SCM in the literature. SCP is concerned with planning. The concept of Supply Chain Management encompasses all activities relating to the supply chain. This includes vendor selection, negotiation, relations and performance. It accommodates the planning, procurement and delivery processes and personnel recruitment and training. It deals with vendor owned buffer stocks, on-site inventory levels, off-site warehouse management, the efficient use of transportation and the tracking of in-transit items. Other issues include duty, import documentation and foreign currency management. A true Supply Chain application package will support all these activities.

2.5 Customer Relationship Management (CRM)

Although the need to manage customer relationships is not a new concept, around 1998 a phrase emerged which attempted to encapsulate everything relating to this: 'Customer Relationship Management' (CRM). One significant feature of CRM was that it focused attention upon revenue generating activities. This contrasts with the more traditional focus of ERP, which is on operations, with improvements and benefits having an impact upon the cost aspects of doing business.

Its emergence appears to be the outcome of several developments in the Sales and Marketing domains.

On one hand, there were technological developments. It was increasingly recognized that MRPII and ERP systems, which focused on manufacturing and related activities, failed to meet the growing needs of the Sales and Marketing functions. Customer contact management, product and price lists and direct mailing were among the first applications to be developed. Later additions to this have included campaign management, call centre services and market intelligence management. One of the key technological issues has been the integration of the different technologies: databases, laptops, mobile phones, client/server, computer–telephony integration. The Internet has spawned new channels: e-mail and portals. With the removal of technological barriers it becomes possible for information to be immediately available at any location globally. However, one of the main concerns is security. Unsecured channels present a threat of interception and intrusion. One of the solutions being developed is encryption.

At the same time, there was a growing recognition of the need to be more customer orientated. Enabled by the technological developments, the search was for better practices and greater efficiencies. Data analysis allows better customer profiling and hence more efficient customer targeting. On-line data entry from remote locations improves information about customer interactions and enables the development of more efficient ways of approaching customers. The development of call centres enables 24-hour customer support. On-line data access enables customers to be informed about the current status of their accounts and orders. Developments in logistics technology enables better tracking of products and early awareness of delivery problems. The assumption is that, by being better informed, the customer can be better satisfied.

So what is CRM? Gartner Inc. defines CRM as:

> *a business strategy, the outcomes of which optimise profitability, revenue and customer satisfaction by organising around customer segments, fostering customer-satisfying behaviours, and implementing customer-centric processes.*[14]

This definition makes no reference to technology. Instead, this definition is qualified in the next sentence:

> *By definition then CRM technologies enable greater customer insight, increased customer access, more effective interactions and integration throughout all customer channels and back-office enterprise functions.*

Whilst Gartner Inc. distinguishes between CRM and the enabling technologies, popular usage suggests that CRM appears to be all things to all people.

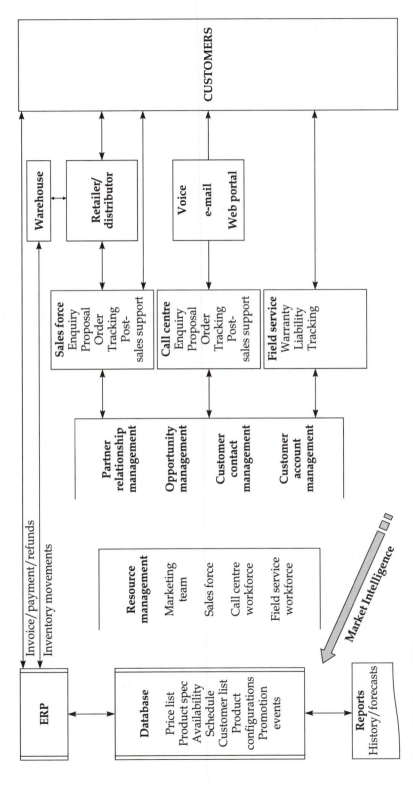

Figure 2.2 Scoping CRM

CRM can be described as the development and implementation of a strategy for handling interactions with past, existing or future customers. It covers all customer-orientated activities from potential market identification through to customer loyalty retention. It is technology enabled and involves data capture and analysis, information generation and distribution, and customer-orientated activity. Figure 2.2 attempts to model elements of CRM. It identifies a central database, integration with an ERP system and different channels of interaction. It recognizes different participants and the facility to manage these participants. Finally, it distinguishes different emphasis in dealing with the customer, including account management and opportunity exploitation.

There are a number of potential benefits in following a CRM route. Increased automation facilitates better use of existing resources, better quality of information, faster response time, improved customer targeting, better customer retention and increased sales. However, implementation of a CRM system has been described as 'not easy'[15] with expectations often not being met. Reasons for failure[16,17] include excessive expectations, lack of understanding of what CRM is, the misconception that CRM is a technical solution, not a business solution, poor requirements definition, required data not being captured or being inaccessible, lack of sponsorship, politics and inadequate attention to employees. Nevertheless, whilst the technology enables the supplier to know all about the customer, it remains to be seen whether this is at the expense of the old adage 'know your customer'.

2.6 Convergence

The evolution of ERP has been paralleled by more recent developments in Business Intelligence, EDI, e-commerce, SCP and CRM. Whilst each has had its own focus, there is a growing complementarity between them. This has arisen from the recognition that the prospective client, when thinking about a new ERP system will not be thinking solely about a production system. Indeed, production may be completely absent and a host of service-orientated activities may form the core business activities. Furthermore, the client will be giving consideration to functionality which will enhance both customer and supplier relationships. His attention will dwell upon opportunities offered by the Internet. He will also consider how data can be used to provide a better understanding of what is going on.

Vendors, recognizing this, are developing their product portfolios to meet these requirements. Whilst the strengths of specific products still tend to lie in their traditional areas, other functionality or integration with 'partner's' applications are offered. A 'complete solution' is presented. Whilst ERP vendors are extending their spread into the domains held by CRM and SCP vendors, these vendors are likewise extending into the domain of the ERP vendors. ERP has become a melting pot accommodating a wide range of enterprise application software.

The present generation

3.1 ERP or enterprise application software

The focus of this book may dwell upon the acronym ERP, but examination of what ERP represents reveals that it extends well beyond the simple Materials Requirements Planning (MRP) systems in which ERP has its roots. ERP has expanded both in terms of how the data is handled and the context in which the application is applied. Applications have extended beyond manufacturing to cater for all industrial activities. Furthermore, whilst ERP has addressed both customer-facing and supply chain processes, this has tended to be on a rather basic level allowing niche vendors to emerge with their specialist offerings, e.g. SCP (Section 2.4) and CRM (Section 2.5). In reaction to this, ERP vendors have developed their own offerings as integrated solutions. Technological advances are enabling vendors to push the boundaries of what ERP can support in terms of function-ality and interface. The advent of the World Wide Web has created new opportunities by opening up a new channel for people to interact, particularly from remote locations. The newly commercialized Wireless Application Protocol (WAP) offers the potential for access to the ERP application whilst on the move. What is emerging is a suite of technology enabled software which is directed at any application within an enterprise. A model of this is presented in Figure 3.1.

Since the scope of the software application is enterprise-wide, a question can be asked about its impact upon the organization. It can be argued that it is mandatory to have an integrated

Business strategy		
Supply chain management	**Enterprise management**	**Customer management**
Procurement	Research & development	Marketing intelligence
Supply interface	Product development/ design for operations	Sales management
Logistics/distribution		Customer interface
Warehouse	Operations planning and control	Self-service
Transportation	Inventory and asset management	Customer care
Planning		Call centre
	Financial management	Customization
	Human resource management	
e-Commerce strategy		
Enabling technologies		
Networks - Internet/E-mail - Wireless - Digital video		
Desktop - Lap/palm-tops - Mobile phones		
Workflow - Databases - Business Intelligence		

Figure 3.1 A model of enterprise applications software

information system if the business is to survive. If this is the case then there will not be any competitive advantage since each competitor will have a system that is potentially the same as other competitors.

However, what distinguishes one competitor from another is how they adopt and use the application. In this case the application is explicitly recognized as a tool to facilitate the implementation of a business strategy. The business strategy identifies where the business is going, how it is to get there and when. If technology is recognized as an enabler, then the business strategy will accommodate a strategy for the adoption and development of relevant technologies. Differentiation and competitive advantage between competitors will be based upon two factors. First, is the lead gained in using the applications, which places emphasis upon the speed of adoption. Second, is the skill with which a business uses the application, drawing upon the creative ability of the business to seek innovative uses.

Innovative use may create competitive advantage. One specific avenue of opportunity is that offered by e-commerce, although it is still poorly understood, under-developed and rife with rhetoric. The business strategy will encompass an e-commerce strategy, which identifies how e-commerce will complement the business's more traditional activities.

3.2 Features of ERP software

An ERP system is not merely a database with some programming bolted on. What becomes apparent when looking at different systems are the different ways vendors have developed their technology. It not only deals with the business processes but can also provide:

- improved access to information
- assistance for all aspects of the implementation, including process modelling and documentation
- tools to support training and development.

Figure 3.2 illustrates various software features associated with an ERP system. These can be associated with three distinct phases of an ERP implementation: the mainstream implementation, the post-GoLive on-line functioning of the application and the adaptation of the functionality as part of on-going process improvements.

3.2.1 Implementation phase

During implementation there are three steps that the vendor may be able to support by providing suitable tools. The first is to model the business processes. The output will be a set of diagrams which define how the business is to function. The next step is to configure the application to reflect the defined model. This stage involves configuration of the numerous parameters that control how each bit of functionality is to function and includes the creation of tables, the setting of flags, switching on/ off different attributes and the provision of values and value ranges. It also covers display parameters and security. The third step is to produce the documentation.

Some vendors provide a set of integrated tools that enable all three steps to be 'seamlessly' progressed. Thus having defined the model, the model activates the appropriate settings of the application. With the software configured, this composes the

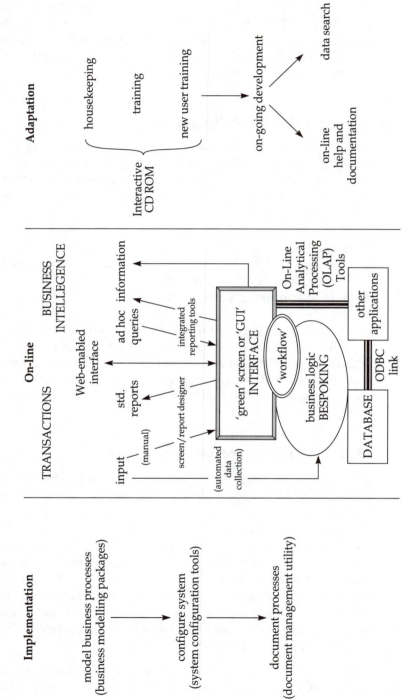

Figure 3.2 Multiple views of ERP software

relevant outline documentation. Despite the apparent ease of using this approach, the reality of using these tools needs to be examined. The client also needs to be aware that once a particular configuration is established it may not be possible to change it at a later date.

3.2.2 On-line phase

When the application is on-line there are many different facets to the software. Underpinning the application is the database. Associated with this is the issue of access by other applications such as spreadsheets, business intelligence tools and other applications such as best-of-breed applications. Partnership agreements and the adoption of common interface standards are enabling a growing number of 'plug-in-and-play' applications. Seamless embedded integration provides the opportunity for the real-time exchange of data. An example may be the interfacing of a payroll/human resources best-of-breed package with the ERP application. In this case, when the payroll details are updated the corresponding files in accounts need to be updated.

Sitting on top of the database is the business logic. The major issue here is whether the client keeps to the 'vanilla' version or customizes it as required. However, when the point is reached where the application is upgraded, the problem arises as to what to do about the customization. It is not uncommon for the customization to be redone. However, some vendors offer a facility whereby certain fields are allocated for customization, so that when an upgrade is made, the customized work is simply transferred via the dedicated fields. A number of vendors are rewriting their applications to take advantage of the techno-logical advantages of object orientated programming. Whereas the legacy systems of the 1970s and 1980s were monumental entities, the opportunity now arises to produce application code in reusable and manageable units that can be connected together as required. The resulting components are small chunks of functionality that can be easily connected together. This is viewed as offering clients a new upgrade route. Instead of upgrading a whole legacy system, the client installs or upgrades only those parts that are required.

Workflow permits a sequence of routine screen based tasks to be technology driven. As soon as one person completes a task, a message is received by the next person informing him that it is his turn to do his bit. Depending upon the technology, the relevant screens and documents can be called up, the task completed and the next person in the sequence alerted. The set-up can be quite involved and subsequent changes difficult to make. Thus it is important that the process is relatively stable and each step in the process is clearly defined in terms of who does what, when, how and in what sequence. The advantage is that the time to carry out routine processes can be significantly reduced by reducing the dead time between tasks. It ensures that tasks are completed, authorizations are received and documentation is available, ideal for, say, controlling all aspects of an engineering change process. Furthermore, statistics can be compiled about the duration of the process, with bottlenecks and delays being highlighted, thereby enabling remedial action to improve the cycle-time further. Workflow is often applied after GoLive when processes have been refined and have stabilized.

The user screen interface provides another layer for considera-tion. Today, it can be expected that all interfaces are in the familiar Graphical User Interface (GUI) format. However this need not be the case, with legacy systems still offering some traditional 'green-on-black' or 'black-on-green' screens. Alterna-tively one may encounter the half-way house of 'screen scrapers' to emulate the familiar GUI presentation. For users familiar with GUI, the adoption of these older technologies may appear to be a retrograde move and cast doubts upon the integrity of the application. Furthermore, in order to enhance the user friendli-ness of screens it may be desirable to design the forms to a more acceptable format. An example may be the case where the user needs to flip between a number of screens to carry out a task. It may be possible to design one screen which can serve the task. To do this a screen designer tool will be used. One should consider whether the in-house expertise will be available to learn and use this tool.

From a data input and information output perspective there are a variety of options. Data input can be manual using keyboard and screen. With the advent of the web, portals offer another opportunity for data entry, particularly from remote locations. However, security is the dominant issue since unauthorized visitors need to be prevented access. Alternatively, data capture may be automated using, for example, a bar-code scanner or EDI. Whilst this eliminates typing errors, automation will incur additional expense according to the nature and scale of the automation. EDI has traditionally been viewed as expensive to implement due to the amount of work involved. A fully-blown bar-code, shop-floor tracking system can incur substantial expenditure on both hardware and installation. This expenditure needs to be offset against the benefits or statutory requirements. The ability to monitor the movement of components, work-in-progress and finished goods may be a safety requirement where critical items in the finished goods need to be traced back to a manufacturer's batch number, so that all uses of that batch can be identified.

One of the complaints with older systems was that they contained a lot of data but the data revealed little about what was going on. Standard reports, which came with the application, would be complemented by custom reports generated *when* it was possible to link the desired field *and* carry out the necessary calculations. The actual task of producing a report required a fair level of expertise, which usually limited this task to the IT personnel. This situation has been somewhat improved. In addition to standard reports it has become easier to generate custom reports. Report writing tools are easier to use and vendors have recognized the client's need for access to a wide selection of the data. Thus, it becomes possible to produce more meaningful reports. However, one limitation of reports is that they tend not to be suitable for ad hoc queries. Thus many applications offer a simple database interrogation facility using a simple query language. Data can be examined on-line in real-time or downloaded into, for example, a spreadsheet for further analysis. This enables the more competent users to investigate problems, as long as they are alert to the dangers associated with linking fields together and the potential for creating mis-information. Another option for users is the use of Business Intelligence tools. The set up of these tend to require a degree of expertise, although their use is within the scope of many users. These offer the user the opportunity to explore the data for patterns. A common use is sales analysis, whereby the interplay of data about regions, products, salesmen and any other variables can be examined and patterns revealed. One useful facility for users arises when the user is uncertain about the exact character string of a data entry, whether this is to enter data or to call up other information. This facility allows the use of a combination of known characters and wild cards to search for all relevant data entries.

Another development, facilitated by the local availability of good quality printers, is the production of standard documentation. Rather than print onto preprinted stationery, it is now possible to print completed stationery directly to a laser printer or to e-mail or fax it with all the requisite formatting. Invoices, orders, statements or any other standard document can be generated as required obviating the need for preprinted stationery. The tools to produce these documents may require a level of skill beyond that available in-house. Furthermore, it may be questioned whether it is cost effective to develop the skills in-house. Once the initial set of documents have been produced, changes may be so infrequent that it is possible and cost effective to depend upon external support. Whilst these tools may be third party, the vendor should be able to provide adequate support either directly or via another agent.

Touched upon above, the development of the web has created a demand for ERP applications to be web-enabled to allow remote access. This means that screens are created using a browser friendly format such as HTML or XML. The data that is to be accessed, the reasons why it is to be accessed, by whom and the manner in which it is accessed, whether uni- or bi-directional, creates a design requirement. Furthermore, access to the application using a standard browser has security implications. Understandably, access needs to be restricted to authorized users. A system that has a public doorway is exposed to potential attack by hackers or viruses. Thus, security needs to be rigorously investigated.

3.2.3 Adaptation phase

Once the system is live there will be various occasions when it is necessary to revisit the workings of the functionality. This will occur when reviewing practices, developing existing users or training new users. To aid this there are a variety of facilities that may be available. Off-line, an interactive CD ROM can enable self-teaching sessions. This has the benefit that the pace can be dictated by the learner. A CD can also provide a convenient format for documentation, escaping from volumes of printed material. On-line facilities include documentation and on-line help. Documentation will detail the user procedures regarding use of the system. On-line help may have two layers; the first layer where the user positions the cursor in the relevant field and, by using a function key, e.g. F1, retrieves a one line explanation. When the function key is used again, a second layer is brought up, which contains all the detail. It may be possible to amend the content of the on-line documentation to incorporate user-friendly comments and thus provide a more meaningful explanation. On-line facilities increase the ease of seeking answers to questions about the system.

Collectively, an ERP application offers a lot of functional features in addition to its application functionality. However, not all features are present across all vendor products. Older legacy products are least likely to offer these, although these older technologies may be disguised through use of a GUI front end and veiled efforts to emulate newer technologies. On the other hand, the latest technical offerings can be criticized for being untested and prone to bugs. One option is to select an ERP application that is relatively new, but has been proven in the field. However, the business or operational opportunities lost by not having the latest technological offerings is worthy of consideration. Whichever route is chosen it will have a down-side which should be taken into consideration.

3.3 Application functionality

A discussion about ERP would not be complete without some reference to the functionality of the software. The scope of what is available has grown significantly from the manufacturing orientated material requirements planning and ordering packages available in the 1970s. To describe each module or component of functionality in any depth would not do justice to the richness of each offering. Instead, the reader is advised to explore the websites of ERP vendors (see 'Useful sources' on p. 173).

However one can grasp a notion of the variety of offerings by considering the following simple model. This attempts to illustrate the integrated and extensive nature of ERP functionality, although it still has manufacturing at its core.

The marketing personnel have a customer list, which they can use to monitor contact. It will keep track of the nature of contacts, materials sent to them, quotes given to them and flag when further contact is to be made. Campaign details can also be recorded with their effectiveness assessed based upon the leads generated. In appropriate cases, the sales personnel can use a Product Configurator at a client's site to put together a customized product that meets the client's specific requirements and then provide an 'instant' quotation. The use of Business Intelligence tools enables the in-depth analysis of sales data and the extraction of valuable insights into the high and low performing areas, broken down by territory, product, sales-person or any other distinguishing feature.

At the design stage, parts lists can be downloaded from CAD drawings and used to build up Bills Of Materials (BOM). As the BOM develop, changes are recorded, providing a history. When the manufacturing process has been established, a routing is generated, which identifies what parts are required at which stage in manufacturing. The design stage is complete when the BOM and routing are released to manufacturing. At this stage quality personnel may establish the inspection criteria, produce the appropriate documentation and allocate these to various stages in the routing. Thus when work-in-progress reaches a particular stage, the operator has all the information available to carry out an inspection. The results of the inspection are then manually or automatically captured then analysed as required.

The capacity of manufacturing operations is defined down to the level of the individual machines. Furthermore, each machine has its own maintenance schedule with replacement parts identified and details about their sourcing stored with purchasing. All purchasing have to do is order the parts when flagged so that they are available when required. Accounts have a list of all machinery as well as any other equipment. They can use this list to manage their assets including calculating the monthly depreciation for the month-end accounts.

The sales forecast and orders are used to determine demand. Sales information is fed directly by the sales team whilst updated forecasts are received twice a week by EDI. This information is fed into the Advanced Planning package so that delivery dates can be evaluated in conjunction with the constraints of equipment, material availability and people. Any rush orders can be evaluated for their feasibility. The outcome is a tentative Production Schedule. This is then fed into the Materials Requirements Plan and shortages are identified. Purchasing assess whether they can overcome shortage problems by securing supply via their contacts. If so, they then raise and electronically transmit a Purchase Order (PO) to the supplier. The supplier delivers the goods, which are received and checked. When the items are booked onto the system, details are matched against the PO, and discrepancies investigated. Any inspection requirements are flagged and carried out. Accounts receive an invoice from the supplier and are able to match it with the booking-in details. The invoice is then released for payment, which is carried out at designated times during the month. The payment run automatically instructs a funds transfer from the business bank account to that of the suppliers and updates the Accounts Payable records.

At the appropriate time, Works Orders are released on the system. The tracking system updates the inventory records, providing real-time information about the location and value of raw materials, work-in-progress and finished goods inventory. When the finished goods for a customer order are ready for delivery, the despatch documentation is generated, the Sales Invoice is sent to the Customer and the appropriate Accounts Receivable records updated. A flag highlights when a customer is late with payment allowing Credit Control to follow this up.

The employment life cycle of personnel is handled with the HR package; this records details of holidays, sickness, training, discipline, job descriptions and any correspondence. It interfaces with Payroll and Time & Attendance. Employees swipe-card themselves in and out of various locations, this providing details of time on various activities and attendance. Whilst the former can provide accounts with job costing information, the latter is fed into payroll, which makes any adjustments for absences or lateness. When the payroll is calculated, a BACS connection transfers salaries from the company bank account to the employee's bank account and the appropriate account codes of the General Ledger are adjusted accordingly.

In addition to the aforementioned ledgers, accounts may also make use of cash-flow management, job costing and project costing functionality. The ability to handle different tax regimes and currencies can be a requirement for even smaller companies.

The foregoing model is illustrative of a discrete manufacture-to-order process. However, the manufacturing component formed only one part of the overall process. This manufacturing operation could have other types of operations substituted in its place. Some vendors cater specifically for process flow operations, e.g. a beverage producer. The point to recognize is that as the functionality has extended into all other areas of the business, the use of the application is not dependent upon there being a manufacturing operation present.

Warehouse and distribution management, post-sales service support and product document management are among some of the additional functional products on offer.

A further insight into the functionality on offer is to identify which niche industries a specific vendor is targeting. Many vendors started out in specific industries, before attempting to broaden out and provide everything to everyone. Over the last few years many vendors are returning to this niche industry focus. This allows them to refine their broad offering to provide a much closer fit with the specific requirements of a business in a specific industry. Such segmentation varies considerably from vendor to vendor and ranges from automotive, electronics and aviation to forestry, energy and beverages.

Our understanding of ERP in its current extended form leads us to consider the next generation of software. Although the elements may be present and available today, there appears to be much work before what has been referred to as ERPII can be achieved.

4

The next generation

The start of the 2000s decade is marked by mutterings about ERPII. This reflects a change in emphasis from inward focused applications to outward focused web-enabled applications. In recognition of this, Gartner Inc. have created the new term ERPII. Another Gartner innovation, ERPII is defined as:

> *a business strategy and a set of industry-domain-specific applications that build customer and shareholder value by enabling and optimising enterprise and interenterprise, collaborative operational and financial processes* (Gartner Inc., 2000).[18]

In a subsequent definition, the concept of a business strategy is refined to embrace 'an application and deployment strategy'.[19]

It has six elements, which are summarized in Table 4.1.

ERPII appears to have discarded its manufacturing roots, becoming an enterprise application in the broadest sense. Functionality is more embracing in scope and deeper in richness. The emphasis upon outward facing operations and interconnectivity reflects the adoption of technological advances in such areas as interface standards and the Internet. Although Gartner Inc.[20] acknowledges that vendors' offerings do not yet meet ERPII criteria, this is an imperative that cannot be avoided.

This next step in the evolution of what is currently referred to as ERP is a far cry from what was initially an inventory control

Table 4.1 A comparison of ERP and ERPII

Element	ERP	ERPII
Role of the application	Enterprise optimization	Value chain participation
Business **domain**	Manufacturing and distribution	All sectors/segments
Functions addressed within the domain	Manufacturing, sales and distribution, and finance processes	Cross-industry industry sector and specific sector processes
Processes required by those functions	Internal, hidden	Externally connected
System **architecture**	Web-aware, closed, monolithic	Web-based, open, componentized
The way **data** is handled within those architectures	Internally generated and consumed	Internally and externally published and subscribed

Derived from Gartner Inc (2000)

system. Its evolutionary path can be traced in Table 4.2. It represents a complex interplay between management thinking, methodological approaches, functional demands and the commercialization of the latest technological developments. One should not overlook the fact that whilst names have emerged to describe a particular evolutionary state, the reality is that the boundaries between these different states are very much blurred.

Perhaps a more important issue concerns the ERPII implementation. If one examines the implementation of ERP, the problems that arise are those that arose a decade ago with the implementation of MRPII. This is despite the fact that the technology is more sophisticated. However, the underlying principles of implementation are no different. At the core of an implementation is a focus upon processes and people. Processes need to be understood and requirements defined. People need to be informed, involved and trained. The selection process should not be overlooked since many of the issues first arise at this stage, e.g. functionality fit, methodology and vendor relations.

Table 4.2 An evolutionary model for ERPII

Year	1950s	1960s	1970s	1980s	1990s	2000s
Name	*Inventory Management*	*MRP*	*Closed loop MRP*	*MRPII*	*ERP*	*ERPII*
Features	Economic order quantity, order point	Master Production Scheduling	Demand management	Computer Integrated Manufacturing, Executive Information Systems	Finite scheduling, OLAP, workflow, e-mail	Portals, Business Intelligence
Management concepts				TQM, JIT, OPT	World Class Manufacturing	SCM, CRM, e-commerce
Application focus	Stock Control	Operational Planning and Control	Operational Planning and Control	Integration	Internal efficiencies	External connectivity
Underlying methodological approach*	Manual systems	Scientific solutions	Systems solutions	Simplify	Business solutions	Virtual business solutions
Enabling technologies	Machine language	High level procedural languages, e.g. Fortran, COBOL		Open Systems, 4th Generation Languages (4GL), e.g. SQL	GUI, objects, components, TCP/IP	WAP, VoIP (Data/Voice Convergence)
Underpinning hardware technologies	Mechanical	Batch computing	On-line mainframe	Mini-computers, workstations, PCs	Client-server LANs	Distributed networks
Electronic technologies	Vacuum tube circuits	Transistor circuits	Semiconductors	Semiconductors	Semiconductors	Semiconductors

* After Don Ralston (1996) – see Reference 3.

Implementations need project management and attention to detail. Whilst one can be distracted by the complexity of the technology, technological issues have generally failed to be a serious matter during an implementation. These comments apply equally to MRPII, ERP, SCP, CRM and e-commerce. It can be predicted that they will be equally relevant to ERPII.

5   Marketplace dynamics

The investment made in purchasing and implementing an ERP system is a significant enough part of a company's expenditure to make it worth taking time to consider the nature of the marketplace. Imagine going live on a new system, only to find that the ERP vendor has been taken over by someone else or, worse, gone into receivership. What happens then?

5.1 An appreciation of the ERP marketplace as a turbulent global pool of software providers and support services

The marketplace has evolved at an alarmingly rapid rate reflecting the rapid developments in technology, the rapid increase in demand for applications and the opportunities for new entrants who adopt the next generation of technology advance. Within a few decades, MRP has evolved into MRPII, followed by ERP and now to ERPII. Similarly, there have been significant changes in vendors. The client now has a range of options about sourcing his application depending upon whether he wants to deal directly with the software house and use their support services, or deal indirectly through a third party. Whilst there is no crystal ball to predict what will happen in the future, perhaps there are lessons to be gleaned from the past.

5.2 Software providers

At the outset and during the 1960s, the larger corporations assembled their own software development teams to produce their own systems.

Table 5.1 A selection of major ERP vendors and subsequent date of acquisition

Established	Company	Headquarters	Acquired by	Acquisition date	Notes
1972	SAP	Germany			
1975	DataWorks	US	Platinum (US)	Dec 1998	Platinium, founded 1984, was renamed Epicor in 1999
1977	JD Edwards	US			
1977	Oracle	US			
1978	BAAN	Netherlands	Invensys (UK)	Sep 2000	Invensys resulted from merger of BTR and Siebe in 1999
1979	QAD	US			
1979	Tetra	UK	Sage (UK)	Mar 1999	
1981	JBA	UK	Geac (Canada)	Oct 1999	Geac
1981	SSA	US	SSA Global Technologies (US)	Apr 2000	SSA GT was formed in August 2000 as a subsidiary to Gores Technology Group
1982	Fourth Shift	US	AremisSoft Business Solutions (US)	Apr 2001	
1983	IFS	Sweden			
1984	Intentia	Sweden			
1987	PeopleSoft	US			
1993	MARCAM	US	Invensys (UK)	Jun 1998	MARCAM was an IBM spin-off in 1993. MARCAM spun off MAPICS (MAPICS application, one of the earliest commercially available MRP packages, released 1978) in 1997

During the 1970s, software houses emerged. In 1978, IBM released one of the earliest commercially available MRP packages, MAPICS. This package dominated the MRP market for much of the next decade. Recognizing the market potential for MRP and related applications, some of the larger corporations marketed their own in-house developments as products.

The 1980s were characterized by growth in the number of software houses. A plethora of offerings were launched, many of them serving specialist needs. It was during the late 70s and early 80s that many of the current well known vendors were founded (Table 5.1).

The 1990s was a period that saw rapid growth in the market, particularly during the latter half. This growth is illustrated by the growth of one company, SAP (Figure 5.1). It was driven by a relatively strong world economy, clients pursuing their need to improve their internal practices and latterly the need for year 2000 (Y2K) compliance. Needless to say, this growth was not universally experienced by all vendors.

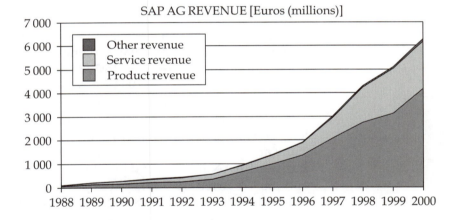

Figure 5.1
Growth during the 1990s (source: SAP website)

It was during this period that a concentration of vendors emerged, dominated by, in decreasing order of revenue, SAP, Oracle, PeopleSoft, JD Edwards and BAAN. When market growth was at its greatest, around 1997, the market share of these five accounted for over 50% of the world revenue (Figure 5.2). The client base of these five tended to be larger corporations who could be located anywhere in the world.

Behind these five, in terms of revenue, was a second 'mid-market' tier of vendors that included DataWorks, IFS, MARCAM,

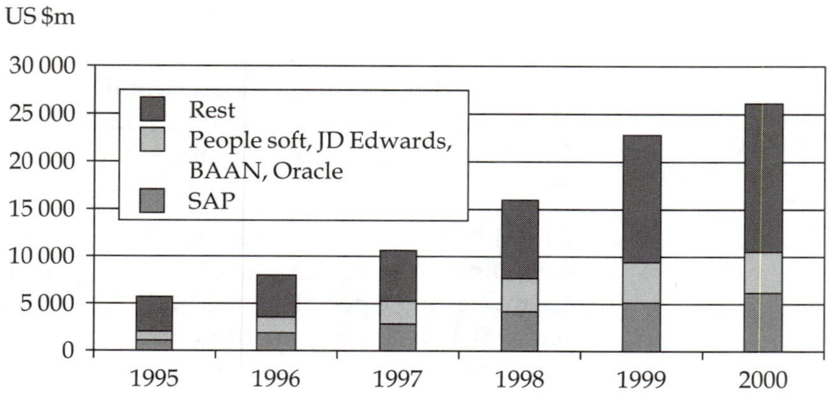

US $m

Figure 5.2
World ERP market
(US$ millions), split
between SAP, the other
four companies and the
rest (sources: IFS, JD
Edwards, Ovum[27] and
Nasdaq)

QAD and SSA. Their client base tended to be medium-sized and larger companies covering a broad range of sectors. A third tier of vendors, which included Kewill, Tetra, Swan, Excel and Fourth Shift, tended to deal with medium-sized and smaller companies covering a broad range of sectors. There were numerous other ERP software vendors but their revenue is relatively small, reflecting their tendency to cater for smaller companies or specific niches.

As the 1990s drew to a close, growth in the marketplace slowed down. Millennium compliance concerns had given an extra boost to demand around 1997/8 but a slowdown starting around the latter part of 1998 reflected both a global economic slowdown and the attention of potential clients upon closing off Y2K issues. High profile vendor consolidation became prevalent, starting in mid-1998 (Table 5.1). Growth during the 1990s came at a price. For some companies the price was too great. Of the five, BAAN hit financial problems. Similarly JBA, MARCAM and SSA started to make heavy losses. The share price of DataWorks dropped dramatically. Fortunately, each of these companies was subsequently acquired (Table 5.1).

One feature that characterized a number of the successful companies was their investment in product development, which could represent 10% to 20% of revenue. This investment was split between the development of new functionality and the upgrade of legacy systems to adopt new technological developments such as objects and components. The split varied from company to company depending upon where their focus lay. The potential danger to those companies that failed to upgrade their technology, was that interest in their products fell away – a potential time bomb. Nevertheless, for those companies that focus upon technology upgrade, their ability to 'get to market' is crucial. Their investment in their future is a substantial drain on their profitability. During the 1990s, this strategy appears to have paid off for some companies, e.g. IFS, while for others, e.g. JBA and SSA, their investment was too late in delivering.

With the start of the new millennium, the marketplace for traditional ERP players appears to have become saturated and reached a state of maturity. The big five have effectively tied up what appears to be the finite demand of the world's leading corporations. They have started to look at those potential midmarket clients who have smaller purchasing capability. In the process they are clashing with the traditional suppliers to these clients. The midmarket, comprising companies with turnovers in the region of between $40m and $900m (depending upon whose definition is used), is the new battleground. However, there are likely to be few companies without some form of ERP solution. Furthermore, many of these potential clients will have reviewed their requirements in the latter half of the 1990s, as part of their Y2K arrangements and have either upgraded or adopted new systems.

One re-emerging trend is vendor concentration upon selected vertical industries, e.g. electronics, pharmaceuticals or food/beverages. This strategy enables vendors to differentiate them-selves on the basis of specific expertise and functionality. This contrasts with the 'one-solution fits all' strategy, which few vendors are likely to be able to fulfil.

The debate continues about the adoption of ERP by very small businesses that employ less than a few hundred employees. Can the benefits offset the costs? Whilst the traditional vendors that target this segment will have appropriate pricing strategies, the tier 1 and 2 vendors have tended to ignore this segment, traditionally out-pricing themselves. From a benefit perspective, there is no guarantee that an implementation will provide a return on the investment and that the anticipated or hyped benefits will materialize. Historically, benefits from ERP applications have generally been disappointing (Chapter 10). For a smaller company, the risk is greater since the outlay, relative to turnover and the number of employees, is proportionally greater. Furthermore, implementations are likely to be more demanding on resources as there will unlikely be the slack that is found in the larger companies. However, there may be good reasons for wishing to go down this route. Existing systems may be undefined, haphazard and unable to handle a growing volume of business. Customers may demand better systems of control. The implementation may result in better and more clearly defined practices, hitherto unavailable real-time information and increased attractiveness to existing and potential customers. This remaining relatively untapped pool of potential clients is now attracting the tier 1 and 2 vendors. They are able to provide business solutions based upon business process models relevant to the specific sector or industry. These, combined with rapid implementation methodologies, are bringing the costs associated with an implementation down to within the scope of these smaller customers.

There are also other forces actively changing this traditional landscape. Client demand appears to have shifted from internally focused operations towards outward facing operations. This reflects the shift in how companies wish to deal with their suppliers and customers. This demand has been amplified with the developments in the integration of communications and computing technologies and the rise in e-commerce. Supply chain products have been available from specialist vendors, e.g. i2 Technologies, TXT and Manugistics, since the mid to late 1980s. CRM is a relatively new niche in the marketplace, with its first mention around 1998. One of the market leaders, Siebel Systems Inc., was only established in 1993 and has experienced very rapid growth since. The attractiveness of both SCM and CRM is enhanced by the fact that e-commerce is an integral feature of their offerings. Both these sectors are young growth markets. Both offer expansion opportunities.

The mainstream ERP players, as they attempt to come to terms with the maturity of their traditional market, re-establish themselves and break free into new markets, embracing all that encompasses SCM, CRM and e-commerce. In doing so, they are brushing against the smaller established players. In the rush to get to market and overcome the time and resource barriers of product and expertise development, they appear to have adopted one of two strategies. The first is to partner best-of-breed vendors and develop seamless integration. The alternative is to acquire companies that have the required technology–skills mix. This acquisition ball started to roll in August 1997, when BAAN acquired Aurum for its front-end offering. In 1999, PeopleSoft acquired one of the CRM market leaders, Vantive, for its CRM products. This convergence of different groups of vendors has blurred the landscape. One cannot predict whether the big five will retain their dominant position.

5.3 VARs, business partners, consultants

The emergence of third parties to interface between a software developer and clients is not new. The 'bureau' of the 1970s and 1980s ran specific applications on their systems on behalf of clients. Payroll was a common application. During the 1990s, as more and more clients acquired their own computing facilities, a new breed of third party emerged – the Facilities Manager. They took over the running of all or part of the client's IT function. This was called 'out-sourcing'. The perceived advantage of this was that it reduced the cost of owning and running IT equipment. Although the client owned the equipment, the Facilities Manager had the pool of expertise that could be called upon as required. As well as allowing the client to concentrate on his business, it averted growth in the number of expensive IT personnel.

Around 1998, the phrase 'Application Service Provider' (ASP) emerged. ASP is a term that appears to accommodate any third party who is involved in one or more activity relating to the marketing, selling, installation, customization, implementation, running, maintenance and support of an application and the infrastructure upon which it runs. Whilst some provide the full service, others are more focused.

These include System Integrators (SIs) and Value Added Resellers (VARs). When dealing with a SI or VAR, the client would purchase the software license from the application software developer and purchase implementation and post-implementation support from the SI or VAR. In practice, many SIs or VARs act as a one-stop-shop, providing hardware, software, implementation, training, customization and support. The main distinction between a SI and a VAR is that the latter adds value primarily through software customization activities. However, this raises the question of who has ownership of the customized portion of the software?

It is not uncommon to find both SIs and VARs in partnership with ERP software developers. The advantage is that it provides the developer with additional implementation capacity as well as allowing the developer to gain access to markets that are geographically beyond his reach. They have played a significant role in the growth of a number of ERP vendors including SAP.[22] The danger, from a client's perspective, is that the partner may not have the requisite expertise of the vendor's application or technology. In this situation, the nature of the relationship between the developer and the third party is important. This relationship can vary from weak 'agreements' to strong partner-ships and needs to be investigated during the selection process. If problems arise, then their resolution may be slowed while they decide who is responsible for dealing with them.

An alternative option open to the client is to use an independent consultancy to assist with the implementation. Whilst the consultants may have valuable business and implementation experience, the Consultant may be unfamiliar with the application.

A relatively new concept is that of the data centre. Reminiscent of the bureau, this provider owns both application and infrastructure. The client, instead of experiencing the up-front costs traditionally associated with an application, pays a monthly rent for use of specific functionality. This can be accessed through a dumb terminal. As well as bringing the cost of an ERP application within the reach of smaller businesses, this approach is viewed as 'the future of business computing'.[23] However, various concerns have been voiced. These include security, data ownership, service reliability and responsiveness. Whilst still a very immature market, as it develops, these issues should be addressed.

One third party who provides a specialized service is the Enterprise Application Integrator (EAI). Unlike the SI and VAR, the EAI is unlikely to support the implementation itself. Instead, the EAI provides integration tools (middleware) that ease the integration of different systems. The technology is relatively immature and there are questions about how this sector will develop.[24]

The introduction of a third party into the equation introduces another variable to be managed. However, it can be argued that the use of a Service Level Agreement (SLA) can reduce the likelihood of dispute. A SLA defines the acceptable levels of performance and responsibilities for the key activities provided by the service provider. Issues likely to be included are responsiveness, reliability and the meeting of deadlines. Where penalty clauses are attached then compensation may be obtained if performance is not attained. Sample SLAs can be found at the website www.techrepublic.com.

5.4 'Buyer beware'

By the time a buyer of an ERP system is in a position to start making use of the purchased application, both the technology and the vendor will have moved on in their evolution. How they will have moved on is open to speculation. However, they will have moved on, since to remain motionless is a sure way for the vendor to pass away and the technology to become a legacy. This and the preceding chapters hopefully provide an insight into the forces at work in the marketplace; how technology is continually evolving; how vendors are under continual pressure to adapt, both in the way they do business and their technology. By being aware that what is seen today has gone tomorrow, the buyer should not be surprised by events.

6 Initial need

6.1 Why

Someone somewhere decides there is a need for a new information system. The decision may be the outcome of a strategic evaluation of the business (Section 3.1). The information system could have a significant impact on the performance of the business though this should be assessed within the perspective of all strategic options.

Alternatively, the decision for a new information system may be the whim of the managing director. It is quite possible that that person has totally failed to appreciate the significance of that decision. The cost of the system, the cost of the time implementing the system, the risk to the business if things go wrong, the cost of putting things right, the failure to achieve the envisaged benefits . . .

Whether one links the need to a business strategy or goes down the whim route is discretionary. In either case, whilst it may appear to be common sense, the need for an ERP system should be established.

Establishing the need provides the occasion to explore and define the opportunity. The implementation of a new information system is itself a big task with the mobilization of many of the workforce. However, if the objective is to substitute one system with another, then an opportunity is lost. This opportunity is to look at the way things are done and do things better. Now the focus is upon the processes. The software may force change in practices so that things are done in the same way that the configuration of the software but is this desirable? If the focus is upon the process then this affects the specification and consequently the software chosen. This difference in emphasis can have significant organizational implications. The IT substitution focus will give rise to a short-lived project involving only the minimum of people. A process focus will involve everyone and will continue on beyond the GoLive of the software, manifesting in a culture orientated to continuous improvement. Where the application is linked to a strategy, the technology is an enabler for the realization of the strategy and those affected will also include suppliers and customers. However, this opportunity will not be recognized if the need for a system is not explored.

Since it is necessary to establish the need and an occasion to explore the opportunity, the next question is, by whom? Is the need recognized by one person or is there a consensus of views? Is the person in a powerful position or otherwise? Will the need be accepted by others and if not can this be overcome? This scenario can take many forms. The main point is that the person at the top will have to sponsor this, so the case for pursuing this route should be sound. Whatever scenario is enacted the need for an ERP system should be clearly defined.

6.2 Cost

It is unlikely that a Financial Director would support the idea of an open chequebook to finance this undertaking. Instead, from a control stance, a budget needs to be established. This will be based upon an estimate of the likely costs. In identifying where the costs are likely to arise, consideration should be given to:

- hardware
- operating system
- database licence fee
- core software licence fee
- additional module licence fee
- third party software licence fee
- integration of third party software
- software customization
- data conversion for GoLive
- project management
- consultancy
- training
- living and travel expenses (also travel time)
- upgrades.

Much of this cost information will be provided by the vendor. Whilst it is likely that the vendor will provide a specific figure for each item, this may only be an estimate. Whilst the costs of the software can be precisely stated, where there is uncertainty about what is involved, the cost will only be an estimate. This is likely to be the case for such items as consultancy, which history suggests is an area for potential overspend. In this case, an upper and lower value, and the expected value should be sought to give a fairer reflection of the potential cost exposure.

Whilst some of these costs will be one-off (e.g. hardware, training and consultancy), others will be on-going (e.g. maintenance). To get a better picture of the cost exposure, a long-term perspective should be taken. A meaningful time-horizon is five years. By the time that five years has passed it is quite possible that the application has been reviewed and a new budget established for additional work, such as an upgrade or the bolt-on of additional functionality.

Not to be overlooked are the indirect costs, which are mainly internal costs. These can include:

- time and consequent cost of employees involved in the project
- cost of temporary personnel to replace those involved in the project
- cost incurred due to other activities not being carried out
- costs related to off-site travel and sustenance, e.g. off-site training
- costs related to the internal resources, such as an IT department, who administer and maintain the system and provide internal technical support.

Table 6.1 illustrates how costs might be broken down over a five-year period.

The annual maintenance fee may be surprising by how significant a proportion of the total budget it is. It is worth asking what is provided for this fee. Obviously each situation will be different depending on a host of variables including the complexity of the processes affected, the number of users, the amount of customization and dependency upon consultants.

It should be possible to pin down most of the costs, especially the main costs, to a lower and upper value and also a most likely cost. However, the unexpected can disturb this picture. Some costs will not be readily apparent and can be overlooked.

Table 6.1 Total costs of an ERP application

	One-off	On-going (5 years)
DIRECT		
Hardware:	5 to 10%	
Software: • Basic package • Additional modules • Database • Third party bolt-on packages (e.g. customizable documentation, reporting tools, web-enablement tools, business intelligence tools)	25 to 30%	
Vendor Maintenance:		20 to 30%
Programming: • Customization • Interface development	5%	
Education:	10%	
Consultancy: Including travel and subsistence	15 to 20%	
INDIRECT		
Internal personnel: • Management • Full-time • Part-time • Temporary/contract (to carry out day-to-day activities to free up permanent employees)	10%	5%

Alternatively they can be underestimated. The danger arises when a budget is set, but costs during the project continue to escalate. This is particularly true with regard to consultancy and training costs. Overspend on consultancy is often compensated for by a cut-back in training. This is not helped by the fact that training costs tend to be under-estimated in the first place. The dilemma faced is that having started the project, so much has been invested in it that it must finish. But at what cost? This raises the need for cost control throughout the project.

Project planning software may have the facility for attaching costs to resources used in activities planned. This can provide a means for determining indirect costs. Upon completion of the tasks, the plan is updated to reflect the actual resources used and the time taken. This gives an indication of the actual cost incurred. It is particularly useful for gauging the costs of internal personnel.

From a practical point of view, the one area where costs are most likely to get out of control are those related to the use of consultants. On-site attendance of vendor personnel can boost costs if uncontrolled or the unexpected occurs. Thus, it may be desirable to contrast the estimated costs of personnel on a 'time and materials' basis with a fixed cost implementation. Whilst the latter may be more expensive at quotation stage the reality may be the opposite.

6.3 Justification – cost-benefits

Once the need has been defined and the costs identified, it is useful to determine what the benefits are and whether the benefits justify the cost. This justification can strengthen the argument about the need. However, the dilemma arises as to how to carry out this justification. The ERP implementation is by its very nature a complex activity. It involves many people who need to act over a long period of time in a co-ordinated manner in order to produce a co-ordinated way of working using a technology that may not function precisely as desired. Furthermore there is disagreement[25] about what accounting technique to use, whether it is payback or discounted cash flow, since it can be argued that both misrepresent the situation. A similar case can be made for the determination of the benefits. Whilst the tangible benefits of reduced stock holding may be readily quantified, the increased revenue resulting from more efficient operations will prove difficult. Furthermore, the quantification of any intangible benefits will prove difficult.

However, from a practical viewpoint this exercise is not required to be and cannot be an exact science. The aim is to get a useful picture of the situation in terms of what to expect. The identified costs are assessed within the context of what is understood about the future and the benefits likely to be gained. With a time horizon likely to be five years, much can happen in that time. Thus, the approach should be simple with assumptions clearly defined. This analysis can also be used to establish reference points or benchmarks. These can be used to assess progress; whether the anticipated benefits are achieved. Furthermore, it is prudent to be cautious about potential gains. History suggests that costs will over-run and benefits will fail to materialize. This is aside from the skill required of the project manager in controlling both the costs and the realization of the benefits. Finally, consideration must be given to the context within which the justification is being used. Who is producing the justification? How will others use these benchmarks – now and in the future? If the situation changes in the future, then the relevance of a specific benchmark may change. All too often, forecast numbers are cast into stone, yet when the conditions change which make these numbers nonsense, this is ignored.

The approach presented here is a very simple one aimed at trying to get the broader picture. More detailed approaches are outlined in Remenyi *et al.* (2000).[26]

The starting point is to produce a simple map of the existing business processes. This helps to focus attention upon key areas in a systematic manner. A hypothetical example is presented in Figure 6.1.

In this example, the assumption is that the business is a manufacturing operation with mainly manual paper-based systems. Examination of this map reveals a flow that begins with the customer at the point of placing a sales order. By progressing around the process, the following benefits could be deemed achievable.

Customer relations:

- better response time for handling customer order queries.

Production scheduling:

- ability to evaluate the effect of changing customer demand and optimize production schedule
- ability to manufacture to demand rather than to stock, thereby reducing finished goods inventory and the potential for stock obsolescence.

Materials requirements:

- better visibility of requirements and potential problems, thereby reducing the likelihood of failing to detect a potential shortage.

Supplier management:

- ability to move to blanket purchase orders and weekly delivery schedules, thereby enabling inventory reduction, which in turn has an associated reduction in the costs of financing and storing materials.

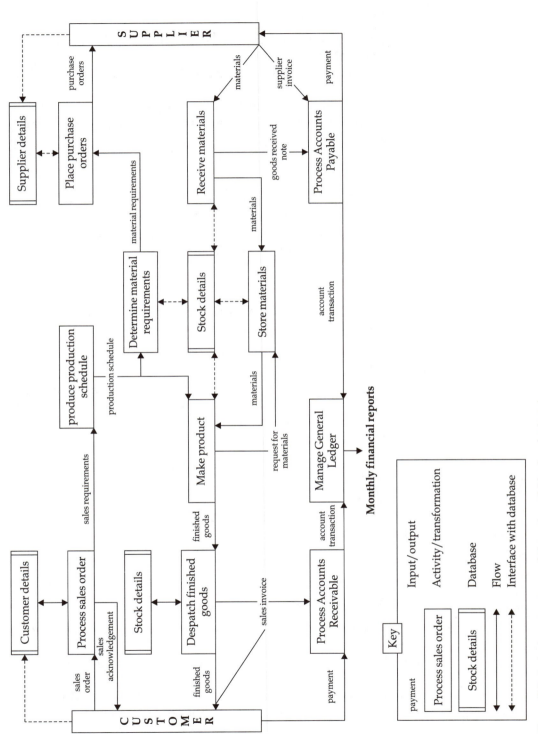

Figure 6.1 A simple process map of the main activities in a business

Key

Input/output — Process sales order
Activity/transformation
Database — Stock details
Flow
Interface with database

SUPPLIER
CUSTOMER

Supplier details
Customer details

Place purchase orders
Process sales order

purchase orders
sales order
sales acknowledgement

produce production schedule

Determine material requirements

Stock details

Make product

Store materials

Receive materials

Manage General Ledger

Process Accounts Payable

Process Accounts Receivable

Despatch finished goods

material requirements
production schedule
sales requirements
materials
request for materials
finished goods
finished goods
sales invoice
account transaction
account transaction
payment
payment
materials
materials
goods received note
supplier invoice

Monthly financial reports

Materials handling:

- on-line matching of PO and delivery details, thereby improving control of deliveries
- improved tracking of materials, thereby reducing the likelihood of 'lost' materials
- real-time stock movement records adjustment, thereby facilitating up-to-date inventory analysis and the identification of slow/non-moving stock.

Manufacturing:

- WIP visibility enabling progress tracking and hence improving customer awareness about deliveries
- better and more timely production information resulting in fewer mistakes and shorter lead-times.

Despatch:

- more efficient documentation production enabling faster despatch of finished goods

Quality:

- on-line data collection resulting in improved quality information leading to reduced quality problems; this in turn results in reduced customer returns and, hence, reduced repair costs and warranty charges.

Accounts:

- integration with the sales, manufacturing and purchasing functions, thereby providing real-time information about operational performance
- ability to handle consolidated invoices or self-billing resulting in less document processing.

General:

- the adoption of workflow should lead to shorter process cycle-times
- real-time and on-line data access which results in less documentation
- data entry at point of origin, thereby eliminates duplicated data entry and reduces the likelihood of data entry error. This in turn reduces the time spent recovering from problems resulting from data error.

Intangible:

- easier and more efficient problem solving
- a more efficient and happier workforce
- better able to be more pro-active in improving the business.

It is to be expected that the resultant list does not reflect all the benefits. As well as those that are unobserved, there may be unanticipated benefits, which emerge from the discovery of unnoticed functionality or innovative ways of using the new application.

One of the assumptions about this exercise is that there will be a change in the way things are going to be done. The benefits are those anticipated to occur as a result of moving to a vision of how things will be done. Often new technology is assumed to be associated with reductions in personnel. The reality is that this is unlikely to occur. Changes in the nature of the work may result in specific tasks being eliminated. On the other hand new tasks will emerge. One of the lessons from this exercise is that the project is not about an IT system. It is about people and the management of change.

The quantification of the benefits provides a measure that can be evaluated within the context of the costs. The practicality of establishing numbers is prone to be difficult and imprecise. The only recourse is often speculation. However, the danger arises over being optimistic about the benefits. If they fail to materialize, this could be because the potential to achieve the benefits was simply not there. It is perhaps better to establish a best and worse case prediction, as well as a figure representing what should be expected. Where it is difficult to quantify the benefits, recognition that there are benefits to be achieved should not be ignored. It contributes to a better understanding of what can be achieved.

Assuming that the benefits outweigh the costs, this provides a justification for the decision to proceed. Further, the quantification provides a benchmark with which to assess the success of the implementation. However, this needs to be treated with caution since the numbers were generated with a limited vision about future conditions. The fact that this vision may be flawed and that the actual situation in the future may be far from the original conception, should be appreciated. If there is a fixation upon the numbers, then a negative deviation may result in the project being deemed a failure and finger pointing. Nevertheless, a positive aspect about establishing these benchmarks is that they set a target to aspire to. If a negative deviation from this target is examined, it may reveal opportunities for improvement. The review of a positive deviation may reveal that the original target was inappropriately set and result in the setting of a more realistic target.

From this review of benefits, it should be appreciated that the value of the system is not in the technology itself but in the way that the technology is used.[27] This important point reveals the opportunity presented for the technology to be viewed as a means to achieve a strategy. Moreover, competitive advantage can be gained through the innovative use of the technology, even if the competition has the same or 'better' technology. Thus it makes sense to consider the application within the context of a business strategy.

7 Requirements definition

Defining requirements can be an involved and time-consuming affair where every detail is captured and presented in a voluminous document. This assumes that, during the course of the definition, processes do not change and, if they do change, the requirements are updated, assuming of course that you are aware that a change has occurred. However, it is unlikely that processes remain static. Instead, changes will be on-going, in response to demands from customers, efforts to resolve problems that occur, changes in personnel, efforts to improve the way things are done, or whatever. Change can occur for any number of reasons and can be small or large in detail and in effect. Furthermore, keeping track of all changes is very difficult. The question then arises as to the value of such a detailed requirements definition, since by the time it is to be translated into an operational system, possibly nine months later, much of the detail may be irrelevant.

To compound this, Michael Hammer[28] makes the comment that the implementation is an opportunity to 'drive culture change and unlock value from the organization'. This is a far-reaching comment in terms of its implications, since it invokes ideas relating to the mobilization of the workforce and the re-engineering of processes. The response to the question 'what are we really trying to do?' is 'best practice', but it must be best practice in a manner that is sensible for the business and relevant to the processes. The reality is that best practice will not be achieved overnight, if at all. Instead, the foundations can be laid, upon which best practice can be developed. From the perspective of a requirements definition, enough needs to be known about what is desired to ensure that this is contained as a requirement.

Another consideration is the scope of the requirements. Is the implementation to cover only selected parts of the organization or all parts? The view may be held that human resources and payroll have a perfectly adequate system. Similarly, marketing may have their own database built upon a commonly available package. The quality department may have a sophisticated application whose functionality includes statistical process control support, the management of documentation, training records and non-conformances and other specialist facilities. Other legacy applications may be viewed as adequate. One issue to consider is the desirability of integration among all these stand-alone systems. This contrasts with the potential impossibility or exorbitant cost of integration. If certain modules are already provided within the ERP system then the decision may be taken at a later date to review these specific requirements to assess the pros and cons of migrating from the legacy system. Whilst boundaries are defined at this stage they are not cast in stone and can be changed at a later date.

7.1 Getting started

There are different ways of establishing requirements. The aim is to identify the processes, establish what they do and define the key issues that need to be addressed. The outcome is a list of issues that needs to be handled. There are formal tools and techniques available that are used by business analysts to define requirements. These include the use of data flow diagrams, entity-relationship diagrams and IDEF models. However many companies do not have this type of expertise and resource in-house. Instead, they may decide to contract out for this. Whilst this may be effective in producing a document detailing all the processes it has the disadvantage that the knowledge gained from this exercise is not resident within the company. Thus, it is not uncommon for this analysis to be carried out in-house. The value of analysis is two-fold. First, it provides a learning opportunity regarding the problems of capturing detail about processes, which will come in useful when designing the new processes. Furthermore, the person conducting the analysis will develop a good understanding of the business and the issues affecting the business.

In order to define a process it is necessary to understand what a process is. Although this is dealt with in more detail in Section 12.2, the view taken is that a process can be treated as an interconnected network of black boxes. Each black box transforms inputs into outcomes. Each input is the outcome of another black box and, likewise, outputs will be inputs to other black boxes. Examination of data collected from each black box will reveal the nature of the transformation and result in it being given an appropriate name to reflect this transformation. Once all the black boxes have been identified their relationships can be mapped out. The resultant map is a process diagram revealing the flow of all the processes within the organization. A simple example of this is illustrated in Figure 6.1.

When this is translated into practice there are several options. One approach is to walk through all the processes, identifying who does what, what materials are used and generated, and who provides and receives them. These materials may be reports, documents to/from suppliers and/or customers, internal documents, plans, computer screens. Each point where something is done is treated as a black box. The aim is to record these details, following a trail of successive customers so that a map emerges of all the processes. The problem with this approach is that it presents only a simplified view of what happens, with the danger that trails can be omitted due to oversight or ignorance of their existence. For the person doing this, it provides an administrative challenge in keeping track of events.

An alternative route is described in Section 12.2.2 as the 'collage' method. Without going into detail here, the aim is for one person to capture the detail of the processes on a series of large charts using samples of all the available documentation. This can then be used as the focus for discussion with those most knowledgeable about the processes revealing the key issues. It provides the opportunity to explore best practices and establish how things should be done. This exercise may well reveal changes that can take effect immediately without much effort and give benefits – 'quick fixes'. Each activity is then defined and the issues required are highlighted. Possibilities are discussed so that not only are the essential features of the process established but a wish list of desirable features is produced. These collages are then used to produce the requirements, differentiating between essential and wish list. Special requirements can be highlighted, e.g. languages, currencies, decimal places. Statutory requirements should not be overlooked as a foreign software product may not meet local requirements, e.g. VAT records. An overview map of the processes can be produced, supplemented by a list of all the activities and key issues that need to be addressed. The collage becomes a useful device when discussing requirements with vendors. Again there is the danger that areas will be overlooked but because the focus is upon all documentation and screens there is less likelihood of this.

In both cases, the routine should be captured. What may be overlooked in both approaches is the deviation from the norm. The handling of such deviations may constitute an essential requirement for the new system. Thus, at each point in the process, the analyst should be alert to deviations and how they are handled. However, one should beware of the danger of redefining undesirable legacy systems and practices. Similarly, consideration should be given to the stability of processes. Are they static and unchanging or are they forever evolving in accordance with requirements. If the process changes over time, then future requirements can be difficult to pin down. In this case, flexibility of the software solution needs to be sought. One should distinguish between essential requirements, which cannot be done without, and those that are desirable and may feature as a wish-list. This enables essential unique requirements to be revealed and will assist in filtering out unsuitable products. This may include the collection of specific data or the generation of specific reports. Examples are the production of invoices in foreign currencies, multiple pricing of end-products or the three-way reconciliation of purchase orders with goods received notes and supplier invoices. In carrying out this task, a balance has to be made between too much detail, which may become redundant if processes change, and not enough detail, whereby specific needs are overlooked. One factor that will affect this is the time available.

At the end of this exercise, the analyst should have a clear statement of requirements that can be given to the vendor at the appropriate time. The bonus is that the analysts will also have a good understanding of the business, which will help when viewing vendor products and holding discussions with the vendor.

7.2 How to meet these requirements

Now that the requirements have been defined the question arises as to how to meet them. One thought may be that one package provided by an ERP vendor will be able to meet all requirements. With some of the larger vendors, such as SAP and

Oracle, this may well be the case but there are practical considerations such as time and cost. The time and attendant costs of configuring the system to meet requirements may be beyond the budget of many small and medium companies. Other vendors may provide modules or components to deal with specific functional requirements but the functionality provided may be very basic in comparison with specialist packages. The advantage of one integrated system is that it eliminates the need for repeated data entry and ensures that there is only one set of figures. Everyone is looking at the same data. The reality is that not all the data required is likely to be captured within the ERP system. Additional data will be recorded on other databases and spreadsheets. However, many applications offer the facility to specify particular fields for such data. The additional fields allow the client to customize the application without necessarily compromising the upgradability of the system. However, with customization comes additional implementation costs. Furthermore, for more sophisticated requirements, it can be questioned whether or not it would be better to go for a specialist or 'best-of-breed' package.

The case for a 'best-of-breed' package has already been introduced. Specialist packages tend to be the outcome of many years of development and expertise with focus on the specific application. They offer a high degree of functionality unlikely to be found in ERP packages. They may be expensive both to license and to implement. Their implementation requires project management in its own right and the comments in this book about ERP are equally applicable to these packages, although the number of people involved is likely to be a lot less. A key factor to be considered is their integration into the overall network of applications. A special link may need to be developed to ensure integration, which will involve additional cost. However, this is becoming less of an issue since vendors are, in starting to recognize the customers' need for integration, designing applications with integration as a feature.

When it comes to making a decision about which route to go down, the preceding factors may not be clarified until well down the evaluation process. Thus, the client may be running two or more selection processes together. Some time may elapse before a final decision is made about which route to go down.

8

Vendor selection

The vendor will provide both the application software and the skill in how to use the application. The vendor will also provide expertise in how to implement the application, which should include ensuring that the conditions within the company are conducive to a successful implementation. The successful transfer of this skill and expertise will reflect the quality of the relationship with the vendor. The duration of the dealings with the vendor will be for the duration that the application is used.

It can thus be appreciated that the selection of the 'right' vendor is an important process. The client will have to work with the vendor for the lifetime of the software. The nature of the relationship is one in which the client is fairly dependent upon the vendor, in that the vendor uses his experience to minimize the risk associated with the implementation. If difficulties arise in the relationship, the client must manage these as best he can. The penalty of severing the relationship will be, at best, the cost of the project to date, which is likely to be the cost of the software and the work done. For many companies that in itself is a high price. This is aside from the lost time, missed opportunities and cost of running with the old system. Consequently, clients learn to live with their partner. However, living in a sour relationship can be frustrating for both parties and hinder new developments. Thus it is beneficial to be attentive to the vendor selection process.

8.1 Decide how to select a vendor

One of the critical stages for effective supplier management is the supplier selection process. A good supplier can be selected in one of five ways:

- the lucky dip process
- the friend next door
- the name
- sub-contract the process
- systematic and rigorous evaluation.

Although the first approach is quick and may prove successful, the odds are not in its favour. The odds of a successful selection are perhaps better with the second approach. Certainly, the relationship may be better, but there is no guarantee that the product is the best or even adequate for the application. Alternatively, the third approach offers perhaps even better odds since its reputation goes before it. However, it suffers from the syndrome of just because it has the name it does not mean that it is good for the business. An alternative approach is to employ a consultant to do the task. Apart from the expense, the consultant is unlikely to be familiar with the business and there is the issue of acceptability of the findings. Does the consultant have an unbiased view of the vendor market or has he some affiliation with a specific vendor? One should also consider what happens at a later date if the implementation or the relationship with the vendor becomes a problem. The latter approach, whilst time-consuming, will still not guarantee success. However, the likelihood of picking the wrong supplier are reduced. Depending upon the selection criteria used it is more likely to yield a better fit with the needs of the business, as well as generating a better feeling of comfort with the vendor. It is this latter approach that is adopted here.

Having decided the approach, it remains to decide who is going to be involved in making the decision. There are various considerations. Who are the owners of the new system? Are they to be involved in the selection process and, if so, how involved? Whilst the feeling that a system is being imposed must be avoided, it is impractical to have everyone involved at all stages. Furthermore, it must be remembered that the project is not an IT project nor can IT claim ownership for it. Thus, some sort of sensible compromise needs to be reached.

One possibility is to limit involvement to key managers and users. This has the benefit of enabling them to apply their knowledge and experience to assess the functional fit of the software to needs. It also enables informal dissemination to others. However, it is perhaps unnecessary for them to have much involvement in the early stages of the evaluation process. They are unlikely to be particularly interested in nonfunctional issues. The person dealing with technical issues such as platform and database may desire more involvement, particularly if that person is to maintain the system after it has been implemented. Nevertheless, when progressing through the short-list approach, this small team may only start to become involved at stage three (below). They may selectively sit in on vendor demonstrations, so that they, as a team, are acquainted with each application. They will then meet to reduce the short-list. The person responsible for the vendor research may guide the team through the nonfunctional issues. The team, as representatives of the users, make the decision as to which vendor is short-listed, thereby ensuring that ownership for the system remains with them.

The key constraint is time. More realistically, the team's first contact with the vendor may occur in stage four when there are only three or four vendors. The danger is that vendors with good user friendly functionality are unduly eliminated, leaving a vendor with poor functionality in the short-list. It is at this stage that the team play an important role in understanding all the issues relating to the vendors so that it is they, not the researcher, who decides which vendor to select. The focus is upon ensuring that ownership for both the decision and the new system rests with the users.

8.2 The short-list route

The vendor appraisal process comprises four stages:

- stage 1: find out who is out there (generating the first list)
- stage 2: generate a short-list of suppliers who offer the potential for meeting requirements
- stage 3: reduce the short-list to those who are deemed most suitable
- stage 4: final selection.

This process can take one person four to six weeks depending upon their familiarity with the marketplace. It may be useful to develop a plan of the appraisal process including dates for decisions and contract exchange. By planning these events, meetings can be arranged to ensure that all those involved in the selection process are available thereby minimizing delays due to conflicting appointments. During this process, a lot of data will be collected, which will need to be appraised in some way. A spreadsheet is useful for the collation of this data. It provides a useful tool to allow the comparison of the relative strengths and weaknesses of each vendor. It is also easily distributed, although this should be controlled in some way to ensure that people receive and use the same version.

8.2.1 Stage 1: finding out who is out there (generating the first list)

Who is out there? Who should I be talking to? There are many ERP vendors all vying for business. The aim of the first stage is to generate a preliminary list of vendors who may be of interest. By scanning through the trade press and carrying out website searches, it should be possible to identify 40–50 vendors who offer an ERP solution. This is a relatively quick exercise. However, at this stage it is not known whether it is a relevant solution. It is only by systematically evaluating these vendors that their ability to meet requirements can be determined. The next stage is to produce this first short-list, of about 10 to 15 vendors.

8.2.2 Stage 2: potential vendors

The aim of this exercise is to generate a short-list of 10 to 15 suppliers who offer the potential for meeting requirements. If there are any unique requirements, this number may be reduced to two or three, in which case the next stage is skipped. The short-list is produced by taking the generated list and assessing how each vendor performs against a limited number (say five to ten) of basic criteria. This approach is primarily a desk top exercise, involving use of supplier listings (e.g. Manufacturing Computer Solutions[29], Conspectus[30], Manufacturing Systems[31]), trade press reviews and initial contact with suppliers at major exhibitions, by telephone or through their website. Basic criteria can include:

- **Geographical presence of vendors.** Many vendors are US based and do not have a presence outside the US. These can be quickly eliminated if there is no presence in your geographical location. However, be cautious, since they may be represented by Value Added Resellers (VARs) or partnerships. In this case, the task is to identify these representatives, which can be easily done through the vendor websites.

- **Orientation of application to requirements.** If the product is designed for the process industry then it will not be relevant to an assembly requirement. Many vendors have their roots in specific industry sectors or functional areas, so their product will be more suitable for some applications than others. Similarly, their support staff will have experience that reflects this orientation.

- **Specific functional requirements.** If there is a specific functional requirement that is unlikely to be commonly available, for example, multipricing or multiple country VAT rates, then this will be a convenient time to filter out those applications that are unable to meet these requirements. Alternatively, there may be specific hardware constraint or database constraint that can act as a filter.

- **Number of complete implementations** in targeted sector over last three years/number of implementations completed in last three years. If there are no relevant implementations, then it is unlikely that the vendor will be able to demonstrate the suitability of the software for the required application. In this case, the assessment becomes more difficult, calling upon more imaginative approaches to evaluating fit. Furthermore, if the vendor has little experience of your sector then you cannot benefit from his experience of the target sector.

- Broad brush estimate of **cost** for a given number of users and a full implementation of manufacturing and financial functionality (or whatever core functionality is required). The intention is to get a preliminary feel for the possible costs of an implementation and where the budget should be positioned.

- **Size of organization** in terms of both revenue and number of employees. Do they have revenue to support on-going product development? Do they have sufficient resources to spread across implementations concurrent with your own?

- **Profitability/share price movement.** Is the vendor vulnerable because of lack of profitability? Has the share price plummeted and made it a potential candidate for acquisition? The major concern here is whether the software will be supported after contracts have been exchanged. A change of ownership may lead to the product being dropped. The effect of this is that whilst the acquired version should be supported, there will be no upgrades, additional modules or other technical developments.

- **Initial impressions** do affect our decisions. Whether it is an intuitive feeling based on observations or a knee-jerk dislike of the attitude shown by your first contact with the company, this very subjective criterion can help to weed out borderline vendors from the list.

The outcome is a short-list of vendors who go through into the next vendor assessment stage.

Reference has already been made in Section 5.3 to the practice of vendors partnering with Value Added Resellers (VARs). The VAR provides the implementation support and acts on behalf of the vendor for the software. Contact with the vendor may never arise since the VAR has the capability of dealing with all of a customer's requirements. The approach used for evaluating a VAR need not be any different from that of a vendor. Indeed both should be treated as a single entity. However, an additional criterion will be necessary, examining the nature of the relationship between vendor and VAR. One aim is to establish whether the VAR has the skill and product knowledge to support the implementation. Another objective is to establish the strength of the partnership between the VAR and the vendor. How effective will the VAR be in the resolution of technical problems, both now and in the future? Will the VAR be in a position to support future upgrades?

8.2.3 Stage 3: reduce the short-list to those who are deemed most suitable

This is a more detailed analysis with the aim of reducing the number of vendors to three or four. The range of criteria used for selection is increased to provide a more comprehensive understanding of the vendors. Table 8.1 outlines a framework of criteria that may be used. The aim is to generate a sufficient profile of the vendors so that their relative strengths and weaknesses can be assessed.

The selection criteria framework created at this stage can be further developed in more depth at the next stage. The main mechanisms are vendor demonstrations, presentations, site visits and third party reports.

One third party, Gartner Inc., publishes periodical reviews of the marketplace. One of the interesting features of these reviews is their assessment of how vendors stand, both today and in the future, with regard to their vision about their technology, service, functionality and general viability, and their ability to

Table 8.1 Selection criteria

Criteria	Why?	Parameters
Functionality	Does the software do what is required of it? Is it hardware compliant? What additional tools are there?	core functionality/range of modules/interfaces (ODBC compliance, SQL compliance)/additional tools/database/platform
Implementation approach	Is the implementation structured with a view to minimizing the risks of failure?	vendor, VAR or consultant/ approach/timescale/ upgrading policy
Costs	Are they acceptable? Do the benefits outweigh the costs?	hardware/database/ application (for given number of concurrent users)/ implementation support/ training/maintenance/ additional tools
Organizational credibility/viability	Will the company stay in business for the potential life of the software after implementation?	origin/history/turnover/ employees/share-price movement
Experience of implementing in target sector	Has the application been successfully applied in the required environment? Will the vendor be able to provide the benefit of experience of the target sector?	implementation statistics/ sectors targeted/clients', reference sites
Support (during/ after implementation)	Will the right expertise be available when required?	nature of support, in particular, local support and telephone support
Reputation (clients, 3rd party reviews, press, ...)	What can be learnt about the vendor from others?	
Manner of response	How indicative is this of the vendors behaviour after the contract is signed?	chasing or chased
Direction (five-year strategy)	Is there a vision of where the technology/business will be in five years' time and how is this supported?	direction/product development strategy/ software R & D budget

Focus on tomorrow

Executes well today, may dominate large segment, but doesn't understand market direction.	Executes well today, well positioned for tomorrow.
Either focuses on small segment and does it well, or is unfocused and does not out-innovate or out-perform others.	Understands where market is going or has vision for changing market rules, but doesn't execute well yet.

Ability to execute (in technology, viability, service, features)

Focus on today

Figure 8.1
The magic quadrant[32] (courtesy of Gartner Inc.)

Vision
(in technology, viability, service, features)

Note 1   Gartner magic quadrant

Gartner's magic quadrant represents one factor in an organization's evaluation of a vendor or product. To complete the evaluation process, care delivery organizations must also perform reference checks, site visits to other care delivery organizations using the products being evaluated in live operations, and financial evaluations of the vendors being considered.

Note 2   Gartner's definition of a market

A market or market segment is a set of actual or potential customers for a given set of products or services who have a common set of needs or wants and who reference each other when making a decision. The definition of a market or market segment may change. For example, a market definition for automobiles is no longer useful. There are many significant 'submarkets' (i.e., sport utility vehicle, luxury, sports car, standard-size family saloon) that have more meaning to both customers and vendors. Each has a set of buyers with real or emotional needs as well as a set of vendors offering products responding to these needs.

achieve this vision. They focus upon top-tier and mid-tier customer markets, of which they have distinguished five segments: distribution-intensive, discrete intensive, process-intensive, asset intensive and services-intensive. To be considered for evaluation, vendors must meet acceptance criteria. Findings for a targeted sector are presented in a simple matrix, the 'magic quadrant' (Figure 8.1). One of the appeals of these reviews is that they provide 'qualified' reassurance about your own maturing views of vendors. The qualification is that this assessment is itself a view and as such is open to the possibility of error.

Part of the selection process at this stage can be the distribution of the specification of requirements (Chapter 7) to vendors for their initial reaction. The client is looking for problem areas. However, beware of exaggerated claims about meeting specific requirements. In critical functional areas it is advisable that the vendor demonstrates how requirements are being met, whether at this stage or the next.

As mentioned in Section 8.1, those involved in the process of deciding the vendor may wish to be involved in these presentations/demonstrations. The format can be informal with the agenda open. It is here that functional requirements can be investigated. The aim is to enable the client to learn about the vendor and the product and service offerings. These meetings should be prepared with a view to seeking answers to the criteria listed. In view of the volume of information gleaned about each vendor, it is necessary to be systematic about recording details. This is particularly important for functionality since confusion can quickly set in about which application did what. Also, attention should be paid to the way in which the vendor responds to queries. This is possibly indicative of the relationship during the implementation. Similarly, the response to the question 'Why should we go with you?' may reveal how the vendor perceives himself and again provide insight into any future relationship.

This stage is completed with the selection of three or four vendors to evaluate in further detail.

8.2.4 Stage 4: the final selection

This final stage is aimed at selecting a vendor. Two features characterize this stage: detail and involvement of people.

This is the time when the opportunity exists to find out everything about the vendors and their products and services. It is better to find out about weaknesses now than after selection.

It is also the time when others need to be actively involved. It is necessary to instil a sense of ownership for the selection into those who will have responsibility for implementing and using the system. If problems arise at a later date, people who are involved with the system should not be in the position of saying 'Well, I did not choose this system'. Furthermore, these people will be able to handle questions about functionality in areas familiar to them.

Tasks include the issuing of an Invitation To Tender, the organization of presentations and demonstrations, the collation and synthesis of views and the management of the decision-making process. The key role of those involved in demonstrations is to evaluate the functionality of the software. This needs to be done in such a way that the relative merits of the different packages can be compared.

One suggestion is that the client prepares a fixed agenda for a vendor demonstration. This agenda is given to each of the vendors, which they must adhere to. The aim is to enable a 'like for like' comparison of how each vendor's functionality performs when carrying out specified tasks. Key functional issues identify what must be demonstrated. These issues will not be concerned with routine tasks that are 'standard' on the applications. Instead, they will be concerned with specific tasks that are likely to differentiate the business from other businesses. Examples are, the handling of duty in order to claim relief, the use of multiple prices, the option to use standard cost and activity based costing in different departments, the ability to issue consolidated invoices to customers. The agenda will be issued to the vendor in sufficient time for them to prepare the demonstration with the request that the demonstration uses the customer's data. This data can be provided to the vendor in an electronic format. In this way, the onlookers can be more familiar with what they are seeing and issues relating to the format of the customer's data are highlighted. On the day(s) of the demonstration, each of the people receiving the demonstration are given a specially designed assessment sheet upon which they can record their views. This helps them to recall differences between the packages and not to confuse them. When all the demonstrations have been completed, these sheets are then used to establish the relative merits of the packages in terms of functionality. This may take the form of a group discussion or a separate analysis of all the sheets, the findings of which are disseminated in a report.

The final task is the process of making a decision about which vendor to partner. How this decision is made will reflect the nature of the organization. As discussed in Section 8.1, it may be made by one person or by a group. One point to remember is that it may be desirable to consider who has ownership of the decision and whether this will later affect the right people, the users, from having ownership of their system. When this decision is being made, attention focuses upon the selection criteria. These build upon those outlined in Table 8.1 and are examined in the following sub-sections in more detail.

8.2.4.1 Functionality

Does the software do all that is required of it? This area is perhaps the most complex since consideration must be given to a long list of business processes. Whilst ERP systems have evolved significantly in terms of the functionality provided, it is inadvisable to assume that all the routine functional requirements will be met by any 'good' system. This raises the question of what makes a 'good' system? Instead, it is more important that caution is exercised. That the system does what is required of it should be verified. Furthermore, this complexity is made worse as consideration needs to be given to a host of other related issues that have received a brief introduction in Sections 3.1 and 3.3. These can be listed as follows.

Underlying technology:

- database
- platform
- maintenance, performance and security management
- scalability
- multiple site networking.

Implementation technology:

- business modelling tools
- system configuration tools
- document management utility.

On-line technology:

- additional fields
- ODBC connectivity
- CAD link
- ability to download as .xls, .txt files
- data collection flexibility
- GUI screens
- user friendliness
- web-enabled screens
- screen design capability
- integrated reporting tools
- OLAP tools
- workflow
- ease of customization
- stationery (preprinted or on-line).

Adaptation

- interactive training CD ROM
- on-line help
- on-line data search
- comprehensive documentation of functionality
- ease of upgrade.

Many of the above issues can be defined and clearly assessed so that expectations are realized during implementation. The one area that is particularly open to disappointment at a later date concerns the functionality of transaction processing and operational planning and control. Despite user requirements being defined (Chapter 7), critical aspects of the detail may be overlooked. These were, perhaps, not included in the specification and so are not verified as being available features of the software. There is a fine line between not enough detail and too much. Another issue is functionality, which, when revisited during prototyping, does not function as expected or is deficient. This is aside from the dilemma of anticipating how processes will change over time and what future requirements for these will be. These deficiencies can be overcome by customization (Section 12.3.2), but this comes at a cost.

Another consideration is the speed at which technology changes. One can be distracted by new technological developments and be attracted to the 'latest' features. There is a risk associated with this. As the first site to adopt these features you would be in effect a guinea-pig for their live testing and could be exposing yourselves to lengthy delays whilst problems are debugged. This option is attractive to those who can envisage opportunities associated with enhancements and are not risk adverse. Alternatively, if attention focuses upon what works now, whilst the opportunities associated with enhancements may be lost, there is far less likelihood of there being technology-related problems and associated delay.

8.2.4.2 Implementation approach

Does the methodology have a proven and structured approach? Are the different stages of an implementation defined and broken down into clear and discernible activities that people can relate to and do? Are there clear transfer points to ensure that activities are completed before progressing to the next set of activities? Does the vendor enforce adherence to a prescribed methodology?

The aim is to reduce the likelihood that the implementation will flounder. If the methodology is structured then it will provide a logical sequence of events that prevents issues being overlooked or dealt with at the wrong time. Used intelligently, the methodology can be adapted to reflect the given situation and so does not become a straitjacket. The methodology should take place within a project management environment. In this way, responsibilities and time-lines can be defined, resources and costs controlled and progress monitored.

Another aspect of the methodology, which tends to be over-looked, is based upon the assumption that effective implementa-tions take place when the conditions within the company are right. Failed implementations are often attributed to problems (Section 10.1) that relate to organizational and people issues rather than problems with the software. Is the CEO providing support? Are the right people involved in the project? Are there organizational issues that prevent the project manager from being effective? Are the end-users of the new system willing to accept the new system? It should be assumed that the vendor has experience of both successful and failed implementations. The more enterprising vendor could be expected to have recognized factors that have undermined implementations. Consequently, the vendor is in a position, during an implementation, to recognize the warning signs when things are not going smoothly and intervene by providing support to the project manager and advice to the most senior company executives. This raises the question of what will the vendor do to ensure that the conditions within the company favour an effective implementa-tion? Who, within the vendor, will do this and will they have the credibility to be influential with senior management?

In order to reduce the time taken to implement an ERP solution, some vendors are offering fast track implementation. This approach adopts a pre-configured software solution relevant to the specific industry. It is unlikely that this will match a client's processes exactly. Since the software is preconfigured, processes need to be modified to match the configuration. The time-saving is gained at the expense of being locked into processes that may not be ideal for the business. However, the mismatch may causes inconveniences that are trivial to the overall benefits. This option needs to be cautiously evaluated, paying particular attention to process differences.

8.2.4.3 Support (during/after implementation)

It is extremely unlikely that anyone would consider acquiring a software application and implementing it without the assistance of the vendor or his representative. Instead, the support given by the vendor will include the transfer of knowledge about the application, guidance on the implementation and resolution of problems. This dependency upon the vendor raises a variety of issues about the manner of their relationship with the client and the nature of all contact. The relevant vendor personnel have to be accessible when the need arises. Issues to be considered include:

- Where is the nearest office location? Are consultants charging mileage from their home location or from the nearest office location? What is the travel-time rate? Is there a local pool of support that can come on-site at very short notice if there is a problem?
- Who is assigned to the project as project manager and as consultant? What is their experience of the software and applications? The client does not want a consultant whose lack of familiarity with the software results in errors and delays.
- What are the hours of the telephone help-desk? What issues can they deal with? Is there any provision for out-off hours coverage?
- Is there a dial-in facility for the vendor to access the application remotely?
- If problems do not get resolved what is the escalation route?
- What is the upgrade policy and process? How is this supported?
- What are the views of existing clients about the service they have received from the vendor?

8.2.4.4 Costs revisited

The issue of costs has already been introduced in Section 6.2, but from a justification and benefit perspective. The main question at this stage is not whether the client can afford the system, but what the client is getting for his money. From the first discussions with vendors, a picture will have been forming of the likely costs. It is during this final stage of the selection process that the finer details about costs are gathered. By this stage, a fairly clear picture should be forming of requirements and how they are to be met. Care needs to be taken to compare like for like. The breakdown, as presented in Section 6.2, provides a useful framework for categorizing the gathered information:

- hardware
- operating system
- database licence fee
- core software licence fee
- additional module licence fee
- third party software licence fee
- integration of third party software
- software customization
- data conversion for GoLive
- project management
- consultancy
- training
- living and travel expenses (also travel time)
- upgrades.

It is quite likely that there will be only marginal differences between the costs of the final short-listed vendors.

Specific points to note include the following: there may be an option for licence fees to be for a fixed number of concurrent users rather than named users. The former is likely to be the cheaper and more flexible option. The amount allocated to training tends to be conservative. Since one of the main weaknesses of an implementation is espoused to be lack of training, this suggests that training budgets should be significantly increased to accommodate the unknown. Do not forget the annual maintenance fee, which covers help-desk support and may include software upgrades (though not the cost of the labour for the upgrade process). Where possible, negotiate phased payments based upon milestones being achieved. A fixed rate implementation is likely to be more expensive, but tends to assure a guaranteed implementation. If there is no IT department, the option of outsourcing this activity may be considered. However, this may be fraught with problems. A recent innovation in an attempt to overcome the high up-front costs of implementation is a lease option. It may make more expensive packages more attractive but this may incur hidden costs or be more expensive in the longer term. It should be investigated. Additional costs can be added if data collection hardware and software are required.

8.2.4.5 Organizational credibility/viability

This can be viewed from two perspectives. The first is the profile of the vendor. How big is the organization? Where is it located? When was it established? Is it profitable? How much revenue is generated from the new licence fees versus maintenance? What is the spend on R & D? How 'good' is the website? These are just a few of the questions that relate to getting a feel for the vendor. The aim is to establish whether the vendor is one you want to be doing business with. It may be that there is a feeling of comfort if dealing with a big vendor and not a small company. Alternatively, it may be felt that a small company can provide more personal support. Similarly, it may be felt that a large spend on R & D hints at product investment for the future or innovative features. By building up a profile, each of the relative merits of the company can be evaluated.

The second perspective relates to the question of whether the vendor will be in business in a year's time. If not, then where will support for the software come from? The unstable nature of the ERP marketplace is reflected in software vendors, whether large or small, suffering financial losses, share-price collapse and buy-outs. The high R & D investment requirements, coupled with the shifting fortunes of the marketplace expose all companies. Thus the unexpected can happen, as demonstrated by the decline of BAAN Company N.V.

BAAN was established in 1978 and by 1998 had grown to become one of the top five ERP vendors worldwide in terms of revenue. 1998 saw a reversal in the profitability shown in the preceding years and a collapse in its share-price from a \$55.5 high to around \$10 over a period of around six months. By 2000, the situation had significantly deteriorated. It was then that Invensys stepped in and acquired BAAN. Fortunately, the new owner gave a commitment to the core products so that customers were unlikely to be affected.

As Table 5.1 reveals, this is not an isolated case and warns the customer to beware. A quick indication of this is the share-price movement over a five-year period, which can be readily found over the Internet from numerous websites. A significant and rapid decline is perhaps indicative of future events.

8.2.4.6 Experience of client's business sector

There are various reasons for wanting experience of the client's own business sector. First, an implementation in the client's own sector suggests that the software works in a similar environment. Thus, it is likely to meet many of the functional requirements. The reasoning is that other businesses in this sector are likely to have similar processes, suppliers and customers, so that there will be commonality in the way of dealing with them. However, this reasoning should not be taken for granted. Evidence is desirable in the form of reference sites that can be visited. Furthermore, as stated in Section 8.2.4.1, it should not be assumed that any aspect of functionality is taken as given.

One of the aims of the implementation is to adopt best practices. The rationale is that benefits can potentially arise as much by re-engineering processes as by using new software. The software is an enabler for the new practices. One way this can be done is through the experiences of the vendor's consultants. It can be questioned whether it is necessary for a consultant to have specific experience of the customer's business sector. The advantage is that the consultant will be familiar with the main issues. However, cross-sector experience can provide fresh insights into other best practices that can be translated into best practices for the customer.

8.2.4.7 Reputation

A complementary means of evaluating vendors is to go to third party sources. These include independent commentators on the industry, of whom AMR Research and Gartner Inc. are two high profile names based in the US. They provide useful commentaries about, amongst other things, the state of the market, the positioning of the vendors (the magic quadrant: Figure 8.1) and future trends. The computing and related trade press is another source providing news about the marketplace, the implementation experiences of customers and also about vendors, including their misfortunes. Visits to companies hosting a vendor's application can provide first-hand accounts of experiences. These visits can provide insights into the reasons why a particular vendor was selected, the problems experienced and how they were handled, reflections about what would have been done differently if the clock could be turned back and the benefits achieved. These can be useful in that they may give prior insight into the vendor's personnel, who may be those most likely to perform your implementation.

8.2.4.8 Manner of handling enquiry

The myth that the first impression is important in the decision about whether the relationship will work should not be overlooked. The precontract experiences with the vendor may be a good indicator of what will follow. A pro-active sales team who chase every query may say much about the sales team. However, it may also reflect the culture of the organization, in which case, those involved in the implementation are likely to behave in a similar manner. If this is the case, then this may give a comfortable feeling that implementation problems will be closed off efficiently. This contrasts with the sales team that is forever being chased for answers. During presentations, do the sales team pursue their own agenda or do they adjust to the needs of the client? The vendor's customer orientation should be visible through its sales team. If it is absent then is it likely to be present somewhere else?

8.2.4.9 Direction – five-year strategy

The answers to this section are likely to emerge at the same time as addressing the issues relating to the profile and viability of the vendor (Section 8.2.4.5). The mission statement, the chairman's statement in the annual report, the R & D spend, white papers and product developments may all provide insights into where the business is going. If there is a lot of activity in terms of new products and new technologies, then it may be assumed that this is part of a long-term strategy to be competitive. This contrasts with expansion into new geographical areas, which may be indicative of a shorter-term strategy to increase market revenues. Although much can be read into the activities of a vendor, the main concern is to be assured that there is focus on the longer term. This is especially true with regard to product development. When it comes to the time to upgrade, will the product have advanced much? What is the development strategy? Is it through internal development or is it by acquisition? The latter strategy can develop a product portfolio faster that the former, but there are issues of product integration together with the issue of whether the acquisition trail weakens the vendor financial position. A third development strategy is through partnerships and the sharing of technological knowledge. If these partnerships are superficial then the knowledge shared is likely to be limited and the bond easily broken. Perhaps more importantly, it is the absence of indicators of future developments that should alert the client. If the vendor is not moving forward, will it be able to compete in future years? If not, then will it remain in business, will it stop trading or will it be snapped up by someone who wants their technology? Unfortunately, there are no crystal balls and what will happen to any company is a matter for speculation.

8.2.4.10 Considerations for prioritizing criteria

The decision of which vendor to select will be based upon some comparative evaluation of each of the criteria. One approach is to use a scoring system. A score is given to each criterion for each of the vendors. Different weightings can be attached to each criterion depending on its perceived importance. It may be felt that functionality should be heavily weighted and that direction lightly weighted, with the rest weighing in somewhere between. As the weights are a matter of personal viewpoint, no suggestion of what these weights should be is given here. A final score for each criterion is determined by multiplying each score by its weighting. These final scores are summed up to give a measure of the attractiveness of the vendor. The highest scoring vendor is the one selected.

Having gone through the short-list approach for vendor selection, the outcome is a vendor chosen because it is felt that that vendor has the most to offer the client. At this point, it may be desirable for the decision makers to sign off their decision, so that if problems surface at a later stage, they can be reminded of their commitment. One final activity must occur before work on the implementation itself begins; that of contract negotiation.

'Closing the deal'

9.1 Contract negotiation

To cover the topic of negotiation and contracts in any depth is beyond the scope of this book. There are two aspects: how to negotiate and the content of the negotiations. With regard to the former, there are many books, one of which is suggested in the Selected reading list at the end of the book. As for the content of the negotiations, there are a few points that can be highlighted.

Underpinning the negotiations are two activities. The first is to prepare thoroughly at all times. This reduces the likelihood of missing or overlooking important issues. The second task is to know your vendor. Ask lots of questions. Distinguish between sales hype and fact. By the time the decision is made to go with a particular vendor much should be known about the vendor, how you can work with him and what the weaknesses are likely to be.

During the on-going discussions with the vendor, attention needs to be paid to the detail of the contract and its wording. Be aware that contract negotiations may take longer than expected as attention to detail can be time consuming. Various concessions may have been volunteered during the sales discussions. These can now be built upon and developed into the contract.

The process of firming up the contract may commence with the vendor presenting their standard contract. Upon reading it, it should not be surprising to find that it may be biased towards the vendor. Legal advice is recommended. The structure of the contract will differ from vendor to vendor, but each is likely to make reference to most, if not all, of the following:

- definitions
- price/payment
- delivery
- training
- copyright/ownership
- software licence
- third party software
- operating system
- hardware
- liability
- warranty
- software errors
- software support
- new releases
- cancellation of licence.

Obviously, the content should be rigorously checked and the requisite amendments and additions made. Particular attention should be paid to the meaning of the words used, in particular, the subtle differences in specific words. The requirements definition and subsequent amendments should be included. The content should take into account all eventualities for the lifetime of both the software implementation and its licence.

Things to watch out for include:

- payment profile: one possible consideration is to schedule payments in line with the attainment of targets and deadline
- licence fee based on named users or number of concurrent users
- what happens if a software bug prevents the implementation of specific functionality and the bug fix will only be available in the new upgrade available at a later date
- what is the process for controlling software modifications and their testing, and the warranty period
- who owns software customizations and the associated intellectual rights
- who has responsibility for sourcing new hardware and what happens if it can be sourced cheaper elsewhere
- penalties for transferring software from old to new hardware

- restrictions on who can use the software, e.g. satellite operations
- entitlements for additional service
- response procedure for problems including escalation route
- escrow arrangements, should the vendor go into receivership.

These are just a few pointers. In view of the size of the investment, the safest recourse is to seek out legal expertise. Indeed, it may be prudent not to dismiss the second choice of vendor should negotiations breakdown.

9.2 Reflection

The approach presented is not the only way of selecting the vendor. As stated in Section 8.1 there are different routes to achieving the same outcome. The approach adopted is really down to the customer. Even if the short-list route is the one adopted, there are different variants as to how this can be handled. It may well be that only stages 1, 2 and 4 are followed with the final short-list comprising one vendor. Whichever approach is adopted, the outcome will be a vendor with whom there will be a relationship for a number of years. All one can do to prevent the relationship from being stormy is to do some homework beforehand. Even then, there are no guarantees that the relationship will not go sour.

10

Introduction to implementation

With the rapid increase in the number of MRP/MRPII implementations during the 1970s and 1980s, came the realization that
many failed to meet expectations. Despite the growing body of
research and experience this view was still held in the 1990s. A
1994 survey,[33] by Benchmark Research Ltd, of UK engineering
companies with more than 200 employees and operating MRP
systems less than three years old revealed that:

- 28% had no measures of the anticipated benefits prior to the
  start of the implementation
- aside from the high number of respondents who had no prior
  definition of benefits, 'at best 1-in-4 do not achieve the
  expected benefits'
- 51% of implementations took longer than planned
- 28% of implementations were over budget
- 68% of packages were customized during implementation
- 56% did not have sufficient training to be able to fully use the
  system at GoLive.

A 'snapshot' survey in 1999 by the same organization, found
that:

- customers tended to be satisfied with the performance of the
  software package this rarely being a major problem, which is
  perhaps not surprising considering the rapid advances over
  the last few decades in software development
- respondents tended to rate their satisfaction with a new
  system implementation at between six and seven out of 10
  with the main weaknesses relating to training/education

- systems tended to take longer to implement than expected; ranging from 20% longer for a large system (average actual time = 12 months) to 50% longer for a small system's implementation (average actual time = 9 months)
- the cost of implementation was approximately 55% of the cost of software and hardware, with training costs contributing to budget overruns
- 25% of respondents did not have enough training
- 52% had involved some customization of the software, with those that made extensive modifications being the least satisfied with the outcome.

The emerging picture is that more implementations appear to be viewed as successful, particularly where adequate training has been both budgeted for and carried out. Furthermore, it can be inferred that the benefits are greater when there is a better match between software and requirements rather than by customizing software. This places emphasis upon selecting the right software. However, one has to be aware that what constitutes success differs from person to person and organization to organization. Success to one organization may be getting to the GoLive stage, whilst to another it is the attainment of measurable business targets. Whichever view is adopted, it is clear that the major problems relate to both timescales and costs. If the tacit or explicit criteria for success are to be achieved by throwing additional time and money at the implementation, then is the implementation still successful? Whatever the arguments about what constitutes success are, implementations are not easy and much can go wrong, irrespective of what has been learnt from the past.

10.1 Lessons from history

Much can be learnt from the problems associated with failed implementations. However, there may be disagreement about what constitutes a failed implementation. A project that goes live on time and within budget can be construed as a success from a project manager's viewpoint but if the benefits fail to materialize and there are subsequent problems, then, from a business manager's viewpoint, the implementation is a failure.

Aside from the argument as to what constitutes a failed project, numerous commentators on why projects have failed, recognize that, significantly, the problems tend not to be with the technology but with the people. The more common reasons cited for these problems include:

- lack of upper management understanding, involvement and/or visibility
- lack of commitment
- inexperienced project managers
- unwillingness to commit resources
- wrong people in development team
- politics
- breakdown in communications
- lack of ownership
- lack of end-user involvement
- inadequate or lack of training
- rushed deadlines
- requirements not properly defined
- poorly defined business processes
- inexperienced personnel provided by vendor of systems integrator
- inadequate attention of personnel provided by vendor of systems integrator.

It may well be that these people problems are a manifestation of the type of culture prevalent in the organization and the way it handles change. If this is the case, then the question arises as to what cultures are conducive to success and which are not? Rather than answer this question directly, the answer should emerge from an insight of what is required of an ERP implementation.

11   Implementation methodology

11.1 The general approach

The approach generally presented by practitioners is as follows:

- understand what you do now
- understand how the software works
- prototype the processes: establish how things are going to be done in the future (re-engineer as necessary)
- pilot the processes: prove that the process works
- complete documentation and carry out training
- GoLive
- review.

Underpinning this approach is the determination of how the software and the business processes are to work together. This approach is carried out in a project environment, has a clear organizational structure, a teamwork spirit and a planned sequence of events and deliverables.

There are variations to this approach. Some of the larger vendors offer a 'rapid implementation' approach aimed at speeding up the implementation. Whereas in a normal implementation, the software requires configuration, in 'rapid implementation' the software is preconfigured to a business model supposedly relevant to the sector the client operates in. In this situation, the processes of the client are modified to match this business model.

The rapid implementation contrasts with the taking of short cuts. Shortcuts are potentially dangerous since they override project controls. The danger is that a shortcut taken by the unwary may lead to a situation that may require back-tracking. This can have time and cost implications, affect project credibility and user acceptance and also damage relations with customers and/or suppliers. Consider going live with a process that has not been tested. When live, the resultant volume of problems may require the suspension of the process and the introduction of a temporary 'work-around' to deal with the situation, whilst the process is re-examined and re-developed. If it takes eight weeks before the process is re-introduced, by which time the process is fit for the intended task, then there are eight weeks for attitudes to become engrained. If several processes are affected then the damage is multiplied. If a shortcut is taken then the full consequences of this, should it go wrong, should be appreciated and assessed accordingly.

11.2 Management of the project

The nature of the implementation is such that it is best handled within a project management context. The implementation involves a series of activities that do not fit naturally into the normal business cycle of events. These activities are of finite duration. They have an end point, after which any further work should become absorbed into the normal business activity. It also requires allocated resource and the development of specific skills. It is multidisciplined and team orientated. The complexity is compounded by the need to involve an increasing number of people over time, distracting them from their normal activities. Thus, the way of working tends to contrast with conventional department-orientated businesses.

For project management to be effective it needs to have the right environment. The PA Consulting Group have recognized the distinction between competent individuals being effective and a 'supportive project culture'.[34] They state that one of the reasons for a failed project can be 'the wrong environment'.[35] This can take the form of a counterproductive organizational culture or inadequate corporate commitment or sponsorship. This adds credence to the earlier statement that there may be specific cultures which are more conducive to success than others.

A better insight into the nature of this conducive culture can be gained by examining the prescribed organization often found associated with an implementation.

11.2.1 Organization

The prescribed organization takes the following format. The person who manages the implementation is the project manager. The project manager reports to a Steering Committee, who reviews progress and resolves any territorial, resource or policy disputes. The CEO or MD leads the steering committee and sponsors the project.

Working for the project manager are the members of the project team who develop the processes using the new software. They then roll the new processes out in readiness for GoLive day, producing documentation and training end users. The vendor will appoint one of its consultants to provide support to the project manager, manage the client account and co-ordinate other vendor resources. Vendor consultants advise about best working practices, software functionality and assist with technical issues. Training is provided in the first instance by the vendor to the project team through either the consultants or specialist trainers. Once the project team have developed and proven the new way of doing things, they produce the procedural documentation and train the end users. The responsibilities of the aforementioned people involved in the project are outlined in Table 11.1.

11.2.1.1 CEO/MD

The most senior role is that of the CEO or MD. This person has two key responsibilities. The first is to promote the vision of what can be achieved using the implementation as the opportunistic catalyst for change. How radical this vision is depends upon the individual and also senior colleagues; for these colleagues should share and make their own contribution towards this vision. Whether the vision extends to Michael Hammer's[36] view that the implementation is an opportunity to 'drive culture change and unlock value from the organization' is immaterial. The vision of what needs to be achieved must reflect what the organization is capable of. Irrespective of whether the organization has the capability to move mountains or only molehills, the focus is upon progress. However, the greater the ambition, the more commitment is required. This is particularly true of the senior and middle management, who, in a changing environment, are traditionally the most resistant. It is the CEO/MD's role to assess this capability and lead accordingly.

The other responsibility is sponsorship of the project. This means that support is given to the project in such a way that

Table 11.1 Implementation project responsibilities

Role	Responsibilities
Chief Executive Officer/ Managing Director	Champions the vision Sponsors the project
Steering Committee	Ensure that conditions are right for the implementation Set objectives Approve project scope, budget, organization plan, metrics Ensure availability of resource Monitor progress against plan Resolve issues brought to their attention Accountable for achieving benefits
project manager	Reports to Steering Committee Provides project leadership and direction Controls project scope Creates and manages project plan, updating against progress Builds, develops and leads project team Monitors and seeks resolution to resourcing issues Resolves issues unresolved by project team or seeks resolution from Steering Committee Facilitates change Controls software modifications Communicates Manages vendor
project team members	Understand how software functions Deliver processes Produce documentation Train users
IT manager	Manages technical requirements of hardware, network and software
vendor project manager	Advises about project management of implementation Co-ordinates vendor resources and third party activities Resolves vendor related problems as first point of contact then escalates as necessary Advises and co-ordinates training requirements
vendor consultants	Advise about software functionality and best practices Train

promotes its importance, supports the position of the project manager, brings into line dissenting middle/senior managers, acts as arbitrator and carries out any other activities that ensure that the project does not flag, including replacing the project manager if necessary. The CEO or MD needs to ensure that the gap is bridged between speech making and action if cynicism is to be avoided.

11.2.1.2 Steering Committee

The Steering Committee is a group of senior management who represent the interests of the senior management team. In any, but the larger companies, having a separate group to the management team may be unrealistic. In this case, the project manager reports to the management team at their weekly business review meetings or, if they do not meet, organizes a weekly meeting to enable the required discussions to take place. They define the objectives, monitor progress and quickly resolved issues brought to their attention. They ensure that the conditions are right for the implementation. This means that they eliminate any possible conflicts of interest which the project team members may experience, that the project manager is able to escalate concerns to them and that these concerns will be acted upon, that the extra time and effort of those involved is recognized, that corners are not cut for the sake of convenience and that they are committed to removing any barriers that may hinder both progress and the realization of benefits. They should be aware of, and adjust for, possible discord between the discipline of project management and their own management style, particularly if project management is not a familiar practice within the organization.

11.2.1.3 Project manager

The pivotal role is that of the project manager. The project manager is the catalyst – he makes things happen. A project manager profile has the following characteristics: can do attitude, communicator, knowledgeable about the business, credible within the company, diplomat and facilitator, thick-skinned and resilient. The project manager is also an admin-istrator, keeping records about project progress, maintaining the project plan, handling correspondence and checking invoices.

The project manager can become ineffective if there is no demonstrable support from the top. The project manager may require people to do things over whom he has no authority. If the person is well liked then this may sway people to co-operate. Problems will arise, as in the case where members of the project team split their time between their normal duties and those of the project. Operational demands will prevail when it comes to deciding which takes priority. Likewise, decisions about tasks may lead to the desire to shift work from one department to another. Whist it may make sense to make this change, there may be objections from the departmental head. The department may already be overstretched and the question arises about head-count. The role of the sponsor is to deal with these and other predicaments. Thus the roles of project manager and sponsor are complementary and essential for success. There are cases of projects that have progressed well and then stumble when the sponsor departs. Tasks that should take days, take months because the project manager does not have the status to progress tasks that the sponsor has.

11.2.1.4 Project team

The project manager needs to build a team of people. Their task will be to understand the existing processes, learn how to use the software and determine how things should be done using the new information system. Team members can be part-time or full-time depending upon the demands of the business and the objectives of the project over and beyond simply getting an information system up and running. The project manager should hold regular meetings which brings the team together so that they are all aware of what is happening. This is an opportunity for progress to be reviewed, for issues to be highlighted and for problems to be shared.

The nature of the project tasks suggest that the ideal profile of a project team member is one who has the ability to learn, think and be open-minded. Creativity and critical analysis skills are desirable, since they need to devise then critically evaluate new processes. They need to have the ability to solve problems and overcome barriers to how they want to do things. Whilst they may be experts in their particular function this may not be so important, since it is not uncommon for project team members to work on functional areas other than the ones they are familiar with. Unfamiliarity can lead to questions about issues often taken for granted. This can overturn some of the myths that surround practices. Members will have a lot of demands placed upon them. They will need to develop a detailed understanding of how the software functions, pick up new skills, e.g. process mapping, carry out totally unfamiliar tasks, e.g. prototyping and training, and deal with problems that they normally would never encounter, e.g. establish which process path is the more acceptable. They may lack confidence about their ability to do these tasks. The project manager needs to be alert to this and support the team.

The main constraint to building the ideal project team is the availability of people. The best people for the project are likely to be those who have the least free time, since they are already in key positions. The smaller the organization, the more critical this issue will be. There will be fewer options about whom to select. Those selected will have greater demands made upon their time. They are likely to work long hours for many months, including weekends, to cover their normal duties and also their project tasks. During this time it may be necessary to restrict when they take their holidays, since this may coincide with a critical stage in the implementation. The continual intrusion into free time may affect family life and needs to be accommodated. For this reason it would not be unreasonable to review remuneration or holiday entitlement for the team members. It should be acknowledged that people have their own learning styles and different rates of working, particularly when dealing with the unfamiliar. As time passes, the team members need to be watched for loss of interest, resentment or burn-out and handled with care. If team members leave the company, bringing replacements up to speed will cause delays.

Consideration should be given to the team's work environment. The ideal set up is a dedicated room where people can work undisturbed. This room should have plenty of wall space so that charts can be hung on the walls. It should be equipped with networked PCs, tables, shelving for documentation and flip charts. Lap-top links should be available so that consultants can link their equipment into the network. This room will serve as the nerve centre for the project. As well as a work environment, it will hold project meetings and serve as a training venue. This room need not be abandoned after GoLive since it can serve as an operations room for continuous improvement teams and also as a training venue for new recruits, those wishing to upgrade their skills or those wishing to test out refinements to processes.

11.2.1.5 IT specialist

Part of the team will include an IT specialist who will deal with technical issues. This person will have responsibility for the installation and commissioning of hardware and software, system maintenance, setting up security and a host of related issues (Section 11.3). Although he has little involvement in understanding how the functionality works, over time this knowledge may be acquired so that he can provide support.

11.2.1.6 Vendor personnel

Not to be overlooked are the vendor personnel. The vendor will appoint one of their consultants as project manager (Section 11.2.8). This person should have sufficient knowledge and experience of the application and the implementation methodology so that he can provide guidance and support to all members of the project team. He will normally be the first point of contact within the vendor and will co-ordinate the flow of different vendor expertise. These are likely to include consultants, technical consultants, trainers and software programmers.

The organization described above reflects the fact that an implementation is a complex activity involving a lot of people over a potentially long period of time. It accommodates the need for team members to have flexibility with regard to their day-to-day tasks yet ensures that there is a reporting structure so that issues can be quickly resolved. Everyone should be clear about their responsibilities. Communication is paramount. Whilst different organizations will have different variants of this structure depending upon their size and distribution, the basic components of sponsor, steering committee, project manager and development team tend to be accepted as essential for success. It is interesting to note that this structure is not dissimilar from that adopted by companies pursuing continuous improvement programmes (Section 14.1). When implementations are deemed to have failed, a significant number of the reasons cited for contributing to failure are organizational issues (Section 10.1).

11.2.2 Scope

One of the key decisions is the scope of the implementation. One option is to undergo a complete switch-over from any old systems to the new system, the 'big bang' approach. Another option is to introduce the software in stages, core functionality first then rolling out additional functionality in successive stages. In both situations there is the option of whether to have both the old and new systems run in parallel.

Consideration should be given to a number of factors:

- speed or urgency of implementation
- availability of people for carrying out the implementation tasks
- availability of time for training all users
- cost
- confidence in the new system
- disruption to operations
- total timescale.

Whichever option is decided, it must be remembered that for those involved in the implementation there will be a lot of time spent on development work, time which would otherwise be spent on normal duties. The question arises about how these normal duties are to be fulfilled. One option is to recruit temporary staff to carry out the normal tasks. However, this assumes that the required skills can be acquired.

11.2.3 The project plan

The project plan documents the who, what, why, where, when and how of the project.[37] It is the outcome of discussions with affected people and involves negotiations over resources, timescales and costs and their agreement. It should be realistic, otherwise, if timescales are too short, potential disruption will be built into the plan and, if timescales are too long, the momentum can be lost. The plan provides a guide to the project and is used to monitor progress. It enables people to carry out a set of interconnected tasks in a co-ordinated manner. Setbacks are highlighted and remedial action established. If necessary, dates are rescheduled. Importantly, the plan is communicated to all who need to know about the project, making them aware of progress and changes.

The most basic plan will identify all the activities, those doing them and the time frame. A project plan can be hand-written or produced using some computer application. A spreadsheet offers simplicity and is readily available. Furthermore, it can be easily distributed to others since a spreadsheet tends to be a standard tool on many PCs. Alternately, specialized packages are available such as Microsoft Project. These capture a lot of detail about the project, enable different views of the project, such as time-scale or critical path, and facilitate the reporting of many different issues, for example costs, resource usage and overdue activities. The key concern is the amount of complexity to be organized, manipulated and updated. This is a function of the amount of detail required. So it is necessary to ask what detail is going to be useful. Another consideration is the distribution of the plan. With a specialized package, not all intended recipients may have the required software, raising the dilemma of what to distribute and how.

A hypothetical outline project plan in spreadsheet format is presented in Figure 11.1. The timescale for the implementation is twelve months, commencing 1st January, with planning and the key event of GoLive at the end of October. This GoLive date coincides with a weekend, which provides time for the collection of dynamic data and its set up on the new system. From February to August, the project team carries out the tasks associated with establishing the new processes, calling upon others as required. The company's year-end is at the end of June, so project activities are organized to make least demand on operational people over this period. These demands really start in September with commencement of the roll-out of the new processes and the training of users. As it gets closer to the GoLive, data starts to be migrated across, culminating in the migration of the dynamic data on the days immediately prior to GoLive. Events are monitored over the following two months with problems being dealt with as they arise. At the end of this period, the formal project phase ends with a review of the project. The lessons from this are accommodated within subsequent phases. The functionality that has gone live now receives attention under the guise of continuous improvement.

In practice, a project plan will be broken down into a lot more detail with the windows being weeks rather than months. Additional columns may be used to identify start dates, end dates, amount of work (hours), estimation of percentage completion, lateness, costs and any other issues deemed relevant. Some tasks will be dependent upon the completion of others, while other tasks can run in parallel. Time-scales should be realistic. If they are overly optimistic then the project will soon fall behind and is unlikely to catch up. This will have the effect of demoralizing the team. Likewise if the time-scales are too long, then the momentum may never build up and delays may result from inertia. Having produced a plan, then it is important to maintain that plan against progress, updating it and revising it as necessary. When problems arise, this raises the potential for delays. It can

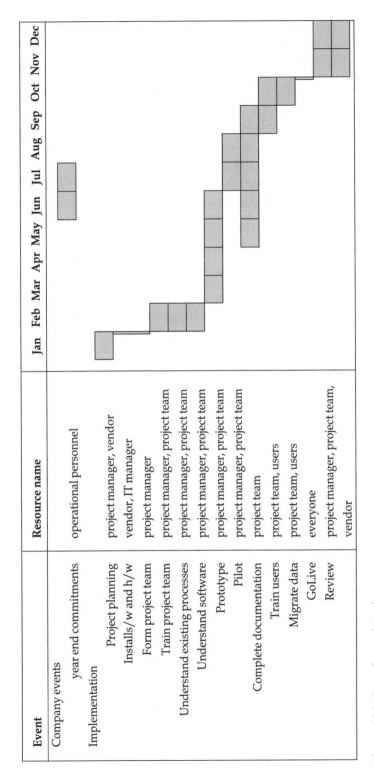

Event	Resource name	Jan	Feb	Mar	Apr	May	Jun	Jul	Aug	Sep	Oct	Nov	Dec
Company events													
year end commitments	operational personnel						�						
Implementation													
Project planning	project manager, vendor												
Installs/w and h/w	vendor, IT manager												
Form project team	project manager												
Train project team	project manager, project team												
Understand existing processes	project manager, project team												
Understand software	project manager, project team												
Prototype	project manager, project team												
Pilot	project manager, project team												
Complete documentation	project team												
Train users	project team, users												
Migrate data	project team, users												
GoLive	everyone												
Review	project manager, project team, vendor												

Figure 11.1 An outline project plan

be argued that it is better to push-out dates rather than not get it right, since a sloppy solution may re-emerge at a later date with a magnified impact.

11.2.4 Budget

With the costs identified, a budget can be established. It should also be anticipated that problems and unforeseen issues are likely to result in additional expenditure. Whether an allowance is made for this is a policy decision by the finance management. Actual expenditure is monitored against budget for the duration of the project. Variances to be aware of include high consultancy costs, particularly in the early stages of the project, and low training costs. Details of consultancy costs should be identified during the selection process and monitored to avoid overspend. Unless the project specification has changed between then and the implementation, this estimate should roughly reflect what is incurred. If there is a significant variance then the question has to be asked why this is. The other cost to monitor is training. When there is an indication that budgets are going to be overspent, then it tends to be the training budget that suffers. However, training is one area that tends to be reported as being inadequate (Chapter 10).

11.2.5 Problem resolution

During the implementation there will be many issues which are raised and which will require resolution. The danger is that some of these issues, having been identified, are forgotten, only to surface at a later date, perhaps after the system is live. Thus, it is desirable that there is an agreed procedure for recording issues and their resolution. Whether this is by use of a flip chart or a more sophisticated process, it should be accepted practice that when an issue is raised it is recorded. When the issue has been resolved it can then be marked as closed. By adopting a simple approach unresolved issues are highlighted. This may reveal that some issues have simply been ignored for the time being. Alternatively, it may reveal issues that need additional support, perhaps an executive decision or vendor support. By keeping track of problems, they can be systematically dealt with. The likelihood of something unpleasant manifesting at a later date is reduced.

11.2.6 Risk assessment

The often-quoted phrase 'if it can go wrong then it will go wrong' should not go unheeded. The most detailed of project plans can go astray for events that could have been anticipated and prevented. It is prudent to carry out a risk assessment. The aim is to anticipate possible problems, assess their likelihood of occurrence and their intensity of impact, and, finally, to establish how they can be prevented or best handled if prevention is not possible.

There are various approaches to risk assessment that have been well documented, e.g. Remenyi[38]. For many, the prerequisite for understanding what is involved in a risk assessment is denied by the virtue of never having been here before. To keep it simple, a basic approach is adopted. The starting point is to recognize that the project has the potential to fail. The question that should spring to mind is . . . why?

The first task is to understand what is involved. Whilst this discourse on risk is presented within the chapters on 'Implementation', it is worth considering that, problems that surface at the implementation stage may have arisen due to inattention during the selection stage. Thus, it can be argued that the risk assessment takes place during the early stages of the selection process. However, this assumes that the assessor is familiar with the ERP selection and implementation process, which may be the case if he has prior experience of one or has read this text. However, for many people this will be a new experience and sufficient understanding of what is involved will not arise until the management issues relating to the project have been thought out, a project plan established and the implementation itself started. In which case, whilst it is not too late to carry out the risk assessment, it may mean that the conditions are already established for some problems, which are currently in a dormant state.

An appreciation of what is involved will enable the potential risks to be determined. An insight into potential issues can be gained by reviewing the main problems experienced by others (Section 10.1). Many tend to be people related. Technology and methodological issues tend to be of lesser prominence. The result may be an unwieldy, long list. In this case it may be desirable to establish which risks are the most important and focus on these. Each risk is assessed for how severely it can impact the project and the business, and the likelihood that it will occur. This is a subjective process and the views of others can aid this. If a risk has a high severity and a high likelihood of occurrence then this requires immediate attention. Likewise, risks rated with low severity and high likelihood of occurrence will require attention if they are not to be disruptive. Cases where there is a low likelihood of occurrence can be put to one side. Note that they are not discarded. This process prioritizes those issues that need attention. The result should be a reduction in the likelihood that things will go wrong. However, whilst it is proposed that this assessment is carried at the outset of the project, it should be regularly revisited. Process developments and changes in project conditions may raise the profile of risks that were previously viewed as insignificant.

11.2.7 Performance

The notion of performance is associated with the concepts of control and targets. Three performance related measurables have already been presented: costs (Section 11.2.4 (budget)), time (Section 11.2.3 (project plan)), benefits (Section 6.3 (cost-benefits)). However, an ERP implementation has a notorious reputation for being overspent, late and with benefits failing to be realized. Furthermore, with the timescale long, it is not practical to wait until GoLive to find out if everything is functioning as intended.

The project plan identifies what tasks need to be done. The aim is then to carry out the tasks. It is desirable to have some indication that tasks are taking place as required and that they have accomplished what was intended of them. The assumption is that when a task is done it achieves an objective(s). Thus, the training of a user should result in a user being able to use a specific domain of functionality. Similarly, prototyping a process should result in the detailed definition of an untested process that meets predefined requirements.

For each step or series of steps of the implementation, objectives can be defined which, if achieved, represent progress. By achieving these deliverables there is less likelihood of problems arising at a later date as a result of an earlier event. Conversely, failure to achieve these deliverables and the subsequent progression to the next stage will increase the likelihood of potentially significant problems arising at a later stage. Furthermore, progress can be monitored in a methodical manner. Each task or set of tasks is evaluated as to its successful completion, e.g. has training been effective, is documentation complete, are processes fit for the purpose?

Together, the four measurables, cost (Section 11.2.4 (budget)), time (Section 11.2.3 (project plan)), benefits (Section 6.3 (cost-benefits)) and deliverables present different dimensions for measuring the performance of an implementation. Often it is only the cost and time dimensions that are monitored. Understandably, these have a visible effect on the finances and operations of the business. Rarely are the benefits assessed. It can be argued that monitoring benefits is carried out after the event, so what is the value of this? However, by assessing whether benefits have been achieved and the reasons why not, the opportunity is created to learn from what has happened. These lessons can then be applied to further phases in the implementation.

The use of deliverables provides the opportunity to assess the effectiveness of what is being done. However, potential conflict arises. To ensure that a task is properly completed may involve an unanticipated increase in the amount of work and lead to it being late. Whilst the deliverable has been met, it is at the expense of two other measurables: time and cost. So when it comes to determining whether the project has been a success, consider which measurable is being used. This dilemma is magnified when targets are misused as a tool to blame someone or to score points over others. Whilst measurables provide a means to assess progress and attainment, they in themselves do not determine success. They merely provide reference points for further action. They are not a substitute for managing people in such a way that they give their best and more.

11.2.8 Vendor management

Once the contract has been exchanged the vendor will guide the company, in particular the project manager and his team through a series of events culminating in the use of the purchased software. The project manager, as with all the other resources, will need to manage the vendor so that everything progresses as intended. One cautionary word concerns the power of the vendor. The vendor potentially has the upper hand in the client–vendor relationship. The client, having signed the contract and perhaps having given a preliminary payment will be reluctant to terminate the relationship should the vendor fail to meet expectations. Consultants may not be available due to split commitments. Software bugs may not be fixed when required. Software links may simply not work. These all contribute to delay. The project manager's task is to manage this.

The vendor will most likely appoint a single point of contact, the vendor's project manager. The role of this person will be to provide support to the project manager, advise upon and agree the project plan, manage the client account and co-ordinate vendor provided resources. A procedure should be agreed between the two managers about how work done by the vendor is to be authorized by the client. This prevents unauthorized events such as unplanned visits or user requested software changes. He will be the first point of contact for resolution of problems whether they are technical, best practice related or to do with vendor invoices. Within the contract there should be a clause defining how problems are to be handled and the timescale allowed. If problems are not resolved then an escalation path should be defined identifying the people to be contacted. Communication should be backed up in writing. This reduces the likelihood of misunderstandings.

The project manager will need to manage the organization of visits, ensuring that visits are timely and productive. This includes ensuring that on-site personnel are available. It is not uncommon for the vendor to provide a site visit report outlining what has been done and the issues needing resolution. If there is concern about the effectiveness of these visits then more formal mechanisms can be devised. This can include the production of attendance reports by those internal personnel visited by the vendor. The aim is to establish the purpose of the session, what has been achieved and what the follow-up action is. Whilst this may be bureaucratic and a sign that there are people problems, it does emphasize the need to make the most of these interactions and highlight those tasks that need to be completed prior to the next meeting.

Other tasks include monitoring and controlling costs. By monitoring the time that the vendor's personnel are on-site it is possible to monitor consultancy costs, a potential area for overspend (see budget, Section 11.2.4). Mistakes do happen and it is advisable that vendor's invoices are checked. Queries should be brought to the vendor's attention for resolution, for which there should be a provision within the contract regarding the withholding of payment. Finally, the project manager should ensure that the vendor is paid, and on-time.

11.3 System issues

Although much of the attention focuses upon the up-front activities of the implementation, in the background there is a lot of work dealing with the technical issues. Tasks include the installation and commissioning of both hardware and software. These tasks will be identified on the project plan but those involved will normally be the IT systems personnel. Technical support will be provided, as required, by the appropriate vendors. From an ERP perspective there are a few questions that should not be overlooked.

- How does the system perform when the ERP application is under heavy use?
- How quickly will storage space be consumed when the system is live? What is the back-up procedure?
- Can the live domain be duplicated so that work can be done in the other domain such as new process development, without affecting the live domain? How many alternative domains can be created? How long will the transfer take?
- What happens when two people try to access the same data? Does the system lock and if so how is it unlocked?
- Do the locations of PCs and printers require to be changed?
- If the intention is to use preprinted stationery on dedicated printers can this be done and if so what is involved and when is the time to do it?
- How secure is the system? How will user access be selectively restricted? Is it by screen or by field? How are passwords managed? What user menus need to be generated and how will this be handled?
- Is there an automatic log-out facility if an account is logged in and not used for a period of time?
- What is the disaster recovery procedure?

This is not an exhaustive list but one that reveals the diversity of issues that need to be addressed. The earlier these issues are identified, the more time there is for dealing with them. A minor detail like a dedicated printer for preprinted stationery may prevent purchase orders from being issued if the printer cannot be configured so that the required data prints correctly. In a live situation, the delay involved in finding a solution as to how purchase orders will be printed if the printer cannot be configured could result in operational stoppages due to materials not being available. Likewise, users need to be issued with passwords and trained in the log-on procedure. What happens if someone forgets their password?

11.4 Training and the need for a training strategy

Training is perhaps the most misjudged activity of the implementation phase. A major complaint is that not enough training is done (Chapter 10). Although training is a project-managed activity, it appears to be widely neglected or is inconsistent in application. Furthermore, since the greater part of training takes place towards the end of the implementation cycle, when it looks like overall costs will exceed budget, training is the first activity to be curtailed.

In order to highlight its importance, training is being treated separately to the project management section (Section 11.2). The coverage of the subject of training provides an overview of the main issues to be considered when embarking upon this important activity. Since much has been written about training, more detailed accounts can be found elsewhere. A short selection of texts is presented in the Selected reading list at the end of the book.

Although it may be convenient to take an informal approach to training whereby people 'pick up knowledge and skills as they go along', this is unpredictable in terms of a successful learning outcome. A more formal approach to training tends to involve a series of six stages:

- define learning objectives – what will the learner be able to do as a result of the training?
- determine content – what skills and knowledge are to be developed?
- plan – when and how will the training be delivered? What resources, materials, facilities are required? How will the content be structured?
- deliver – the experience of the learner
- assess learner – has the learner met the objectives?
- review effectiveness of the training session – what went wrong? What can be done better?

Preparation is emphasized.

Those at the receiving end of the training are initially the project team members and the system administrators and latterly the end users and managers. Others may be identified. Each group of learners will have different requirements. Thus, the nature of the training is likely to be different for each different stream of learners.

A training strategy can be developed, defining the training policy and outlining the training programme. Each stream will be identified and outlined in terms of the six stages. The strategy will provide an overview of the training objectives, identifying the people involved, the different streams and the content of each stream, organized into courses and sessions. A plan will provide an overview of where, when and how the training will be delivered. Preliminary consideration will be given to the assessment of the learners. How can their knowledge and skill competencies be assessed? Furthermore, consideration is given to the effectiveness of the training and how this is assessed. Finally, the projected cost will be calculated. These costs can then be used to set a budget. The resultant strategy provides a framework within which to go about the training activity.

If the strategy is accepted by the company, then the strategy can be implemented. If the strategy is not accepted then it needs to be reviewed. A core issue is the company's commitment to training. The right balance needs to be struck between getting the training right and the training being cost-effective.

The following provides an indication of issues to consider in the training strategy, though many have relevance at the implementation level.

11.4.1 Define learning objectives

Underpinning the training strategy are two objectives. First, is the transfer of knowledge from the vendor's personnel to the client's key personnel. Second, is the dissemination of this knowledge throughout the organization. More precisely, the learning objectives establish what the learner should be able to do as a result of the training. Knowledge may be sought, particularly if related to operational best practices. One then has to ask how this knowledge can be used within the company. However, it is likely that the main thrust of training is upon the development of skill competencies in the use of the software functionality.

The steering committee need to have sufficient understanding of what is involved in an implementation project so that they appreciate the potential problems and are able to give the commitment and support that is required. This is particularly true for the project sponsor. His lack of appreciation of the issues may result in him viewing the implementation as just another project and lead to his distancing himself from it. He may have a poor understanding of the roles and responsibilities of all the participants and when problems arise, may fail to appreciate that his involvement is required.

The members of the project team need to develop such knowledge and skills that will enable them to establish how to best use the functionality for the GoLive and thereafter seek out improvements in its use. They need to have the specific skill to develop procedures. Since the outcome of their endeavours is expertise in their respective focus areas, they will become the trainers of the end users. Thus, they need to develop the skill to be able to formulate and deliver a training course.

The users need to have the skill in using the functionality relevant to their roles. Whilst this will not be initially as detailed as that received by the trainers, over time individuals may emerge who have the desire to become more familiar with the application and develop it further.

Others who require training include managers, who should have at least an appreciation of what the system does. Ideally the project manager should have a good understanding of all aspects of the software so that he can be effective in dealing with any issues raised. A select number of people will require more specific technical training so that they can design screens, generate reports and interrogate the database for specific ad hoc requirements.

The system administrators need to be able to set up the system then maintain it. They will require knowledge about how to handle system security and deal with technical problems. They will need to develop a level of understanding of the functionality so that, at some stage after GoLive when the project team is disbanded, they are able to deal with functionality problems.

11.4.2 Determine content

The content of the training can be broken down into different elements.

- Overview of the system: attention focuses upon the structure of the application, to provide both an appreciation of how the software functions as an integrated package and the skill to navigate around the system.
- Functional detail: the focus is upon specific parts of the application, to enable experimentation with the different options, thereby enabling development of the 'best use' of the

application. From the perspective of those who are applying the software, the focus will be on what functionality there is and how it works. The end user will have a process focus, where the emphasis is upon how the functionality supports the process.

- Technical: the content of this deals with hardware and software installation, set up and administration. It will accommodate security issues, e.g. who has access to what data? It will address protection of the system from outside disturbances such as hackers or viruses. Other issues include database maintenance and backup, screen design and report generation, both for hardcopy and web-enabled access.
- Interrogation: the concern is about how to use the data to find out what is happening. Different approaches to this include the standard off-the-shelf reports, custom reports, ad hoc queries and what is ambiguously termed 'business intelligence'. In dealing with standard off-the-shelf reports the focus is upon developing the user's awareness of what is available and where to find the report. This contrasts with the need to develop report writing, query and business intelligence skills, to enable the user to interrogate the system himself. These place heavier demands upon the learner since the focus is upon the language and techniques for using the respective interrogation tools.
- Not to be overlooked is the need to develop the training skills of the project team. They will be the trainers of the end users. For this they need to have some basic skills to ensure that they are effective in their training.

This is not a definitive list, but will serve to highlight the dominant areas. Within these areas specific themes can be identified which may be developed as courses. Each course will have an outline of topics covered. In determining the content, what must be learnt can be distinguished from what should be learnt and what could be learnt. When there is a time constraint, the focus is upon what must be learnt, i.e. the key content.

11.4.3 Plan

This establishes how the training is to be delivered. A number of headings can be identified.

- Overall organization: there are two distinct phases to the training. The first relates to the project team who have a steep learning curve to climb and a lot of material to digest. Parallel with this is the training of the system administrators. The second phase relates to the end users and managers.

- Trainer: during the implementation, two groups of trainers are distinguished – the vendor's trainers (consultants) and the project team members who turn into trainers.
- People: who are the audience? Have they any special requirements? What are their levels of knowledge and skill? What are their learning capabilities? During the first phase the audience is the project team, whilst during the second phase it is the users and managers. One of the major concerns will be the effectiveness of the transfer of knowledge, particularly between the vendor's trainers and the project team members.
- Location: where is the location of the training? On-site locations tend to raise the problem of distraction. It is too tempting to flit between the work area and the training area. If the location is off-site, then allowances must be made for travel and, if necessary, for accommodation and refreshments.
- Facilities: what equipment is needed versus what equipment is available? What rooms are required? Does the room have PCs, white-boards, flip charts, overhead projector, Smart-board. Not to be overlooked are seating arrangements. These should be set out in a manner that best suits the training. Through the process of planning, shortfalls can be addressed. At the time of delivery, the room should be prechecked for equipment.
- Course structure: what courses are required and how is the content structured? The focus is not upon the detail of the content, which is addressed in the preparation for the implementation, but upon establishing the range of topics to be covered and addressing how they are to be organized into themes and individual sessions. Each individual session has a structure, which comprises a beginning, a middle and an end. The beginning introduces the topic and informs what is to come. It should stimulate interest. The middle is the content of the topic organized in a meaningful manner so that it flows. The end is the conclusion. It provides a recap of what has preceded, summarizes the key learning points and creates a bridge to the next learning event.
- Time: how much time is needed? How much time is available? It is desirable not to compromise the training by working within unrealistically short timescales.
- Method: this is the approach taken which best meets the objective. Since the emphasis is upon the development of computer skills, the approach should revolve around work at

a computer terminal in a workshop environment. This should be complemented, as appropriate, by the use of other methods, which include presentations, demonstrations, exercises, tests, group discussion, role-play and games. Not to be overlooked is self-study, where the emphasis is upon working alone with suitably developed materials. Consideration should be given to whether people are to work in groups or individually.

- Resources/materials: there are a variety of materials that can be used. These include overhead slides and hand-outs for presentations, workbooks and scripts for hands-on computer based exercises, and CD ROM for self-study. With the focus of much of the training being on business processes, 'collage' (Section 12.2.2), screen-dumps of screens and completed procedures (Section 12.6.1) are highly relevant.

The resultant plan provides a tool to inform and guide everyone about the training. It also makes people aware of what is expected of them in sufficient time for them to prepare for the training.

11.4.4 Assess

Having delivered the training it is necessary to establish whether the training achieved its objectives. Did the learners learn what was required of them? Are they competent users of the system? Do they know not only what to do, but why? This will involve some form of assessment that is designed specially for each situation. The strategy should outline how this assessment will be done.

One option is a simple test using a script to carry out a task. A more involved approach is to use a detailed set of questionnaires, which seek answers to specific aspects of an activity. Each successive questionnaire probes for an increasing level of detail, thus providing an indication of the level of competence reached.

Whilst this may be relatively easy for the end users in phase two of the training, it is more difficult for the project team during phase one. Realistically, questions should be asked during discussions with the vendor at the selection stage about the approach taken by the vendors to ensure that each team member develops a level of competence in the use of the application. The effectiveness of the transfer of knowledge about the application can be disguised when vendor personnel do the development work during the prototyping activity without fully briefing the team members about why a particular route is chosen. In the worst case scenario, the team members are able to replicate a process defined for them without understanding how the process functions or what the options are. By the time this situation is recognised, the project may be over budget from consultancy activities and the prototyping may be complete. The learning opportunity is past and the client is left with a deficiency in knowledge about the application. More importantly, the team members will be unable to provide adequate training to the end users.

11.4.5 Review

The final stage in the training cycle is to review the training programme. The aim is to establish what worked and what could be done better. The problems are examined and preventative action established. This should not be left to the end of the training programme but take place on an on-going basis. The lessons are then fed into subsequent training sessions. At the end of the programme a final review meeting should take place drawing together the experiences from each of the individual sessions. The lessons from this can then be incorporated in later training programmes.

11.4.6 Cost/budget

Not to be overlooked is the cost of training. Costs will be associated with:

- trainer's time for preparation, travel, delivery and review, which may be presented in the form of a rate
- learners' (end users') time away from post
- resources/materials, e.g. handouts, workbooks, notepads and pencils
- facilities, e.g. hire of room, equipment, refreshments.

External training will involve the cost of the course and also travel and subsistence costs. Gartner Inc.[39] suggest that the training budget should represent about 10% of the total project budget. Using this formula, from a £400 000 total budget, which is a reasonable ballpark budget for a smaller company, £40 000 should be allocated to training. When one considers the cost of one consultant training a five-person project team over a three-month period and a five-day external course for the system administrator, £40 000 is not a very large figure. Add to this the cost of the end user training and the cost quickly accumulates. However, training is the one area that tends to be underdone (Chapter 10).

A cost profile can be calculated for all the anticipated training. The detailed plan should provide much of the information regarding internal resource time. This profile can then be set as a budget. When actual costs are incurred these are then compared with the budget and variances monitored. If there is underspend, then the question should be asked whether the training that has been provided was adequate. Conversely, overspend suggests that either there is something wrong with the initial calculations or that the training is inefficient.

The budget should be continually monitored. Phase one costs are likely to be diffused due to the difficulty in distinguishing between training and consultancy related activities. Phase two costs, which relate to end user training, should be more clearly definable. However, one should not fall into the trap of overspending in another area and cutting back on the training budget. History suggests that this is a false economy.

The implementation of the project commences with the training of the project team so that they are able to carry out their tasks. This is followed by a series of activities orientated toward the design and definition of the new processes. Then follows testing, documentation, data set-up and end user training, though not necessarily in that order. This journey assumes that the issues relating to project management, in particular, organizational, planning and training issues, have been adequately addressed. If so, this should create the right conditions so that the implementation can proceed relatively smoothly. However, whilst the journey appears fairly simple and straightforward in concept, the reality will be different.

12.1 Implementation of the training strategy – phase 1

Implementation of the first phase of the training strategy is the training activity that relates to the training of the project team and the system administrators.

The focus of the training for the project team will be upon understanding the functionality of the software. Training on such subjects as best practices, process mapping, training skills and documentation may be provided by the vendor, but this will vary from vendor to vendor. A local higher educational establishment or other training organization may be able to fulfil any gaps. The training of the system administrators will focus upon technical aspects of system installation, maintenance, report writing and any other identified issues.

The objective of the training is to transfer knowledge and skills about the application, implementation practices and operational best practices from the external trainers to designated internal personnel. Whilst most of this will be done in more formal proceedings, the transfer of knowledge about the software functionality tends to be done on a more informal basis. However, since this transfer of knowledge about the functionality need not be effectual, it is worth examining this specific area more closely.

12.1.1 Content – understand application functionality

Team members' understanding of the application functionality is critical for the effective development and introduction of new processes. Without it, it becomes impossible to make the most of what is an expensive investment.

Whilst the pre-sales demonstrations will promote the merits of the functionality of the software, its drawbacks may be withheld.

The first true exposure to the software comes when it becomes necessary to make the functionality do what is required of it. There are various levels of knowledge and skills required by the project team in order for them to develop business processes that utilize the software. Each member requires knowledge about:

- how to navigate around the system, and
- the detail of the functionality of concern.

Each member needs to develop skill in being able to evaluate the different ways the functionality operates in order to establish what is best for the business.

The first problem is navigation. At first sight, the range of menu options can seem daunting. However, this can be overcome by developing a general awareness of what each set of functions does and how they fit together. If the menu structure has been designed with a bit of thought and is organized in a sequential manner reflecting the flow of processes within a business, then navigation can be more easily picked up. The likely delivery mode for this introduction is a formal group workshop. Points to consider include the level of detail presented and the content tailored to match processes relevant to the business.

The next problem relates to the specific functionality of interest. How can one understand how it works? The vendor's consultants should be the experts on how the software functions. It should be expected that these consultants will sit with team members individually, going though the screens and fields for the processes of interest. This training mode tends to be hands-on.

This is an ideal opportunity for the team members to learn. However, they may not have sufficient skills to learn effectively. They may listen and attempt to remember, but fail to take notes. When, at a later date they try to recall the session they are unable to remember and the session needs to be repeated. The simple technique of taking detailed notes helps to overcome this. Screen dumps are useful for capturing screen information and, when annotated, provide a useful reference for future use. Attention needs to be paid to details, in particular, quirks that tend not to be documented. Indeed documentation, whether on-line or as hardcopy manuals, may be unhelpful. Its content may be lacking or unclear.

It may well be that the same issues are revisited on several occasions until familiarity is gained. In time, each person should build up a good understanding about specific parts of the application. Their aim is to be able to experiment with different ways of using the software and to transfer this knowledge to others. These key users are responsible for ensuring that they learn as much as they can about the functionality.

If there is concern about whether project team members are developing the required knowledge and skills, then it may be desirable to assess them. How this is done should be established in consultation with the vendor, as that is where the expertise resides. However, gaps in a person's knowledge and skills will become readily apparent as he starts to try and work with the application on his own. It would be expected that this person would attempt to fill these gaps as they reveal themselves at the earliest opportunity.

12.1.2 Planning

Despite the informal nature of some of this training, it can all be planned. Dates can be established and people and locations organized. The emphasis of this phase is upon organizing and planning the training. The delivery is carried out by external trainers.

The training is likely to comprise a mixture of formal workshops in a group environment and informal individual sessions. Most of the training will take place at the client's site in the project team room and will be delivered by the vendor.

However, it is inevitable that some training will be off-site at formal 'public' classes provided by the vendor. As these will have set dates and, if popular, will be quickly booked up, it is important to identify the relevant courses as quickly as possible and attempt to book places on the most convenient dates. Unfortunately, if the class is booked up and the next class is not scheduled for three months, this may prevent individuals from being able to carry out certain tasks. It may be possible to negotiate a place on the date required. Alternatively, a private session may be organized, although this will be significantly more expensive if only one person is being trained.

One specific area that should be addressed in the plan is the technical training on report writing, query language and third party Business Intelligence tools. The timing of these events should reflect the anticipated use of these facilities. Whilst report writing and query skills may be required at some stage during the implementation, the use of Business Intelligence tools may not be required until some point after GoLive. There is a danger that someone receives training then does not use the skills or knowledge until some later date, when much of the content has been forgotten. More than one person should develop these skills as this reduces dependency upon that one person and prevents delays arising because of that person's other commitments.

When completed, this training plan will become part of the project implementation plan and be monitored accordingly.

12.2 Define processes

One of the core implementation activities is that of defining and developing the new processes. This is a creative stage and draws upon knowledge about existing practices, best practice and the functionality of the ERP application. Also required is the ability to think about practices in terms of processes and not as an array of isolated activities. A process orientation improves the likelihood that there is flow between interacting activities and that all issues are addressed. However, to think in terms of processes requires some understanding of what a process is.

12.2.1 A theoretical framework

There are different ways to think about the processes found within a business. The one adopted here is based on a conceptual framework developed in Harwood (1996).[40]

This framework commences with the view that a business is a regulated process. This process can be defined as purposeful activity. It involves the transformation of inputs (resources) into outcomes (products or services). Regulation of the process reduces the likelihood that unacceptable outcomes are produced and thereby increases the likelihood of acceptable outcomes being produced. However, external disturbances can disrupt the effectiveness of this regulated process. A simple model of this is presented in Figure 12.1.

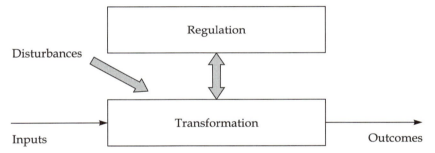

Figure 12.1
The black box view of a transformation

Examination of a process reveals four elements (Figure 12.2): transformation, interactions, individual and technology. The network of interacting transformations defines the business structure. However, people will perceive this structure in different ways. They will not see nor necessarily appreciate all the transformation and interactions that take place. Different structures may be discerned: reporting structures, process structures and informal networks. This becomes potentially

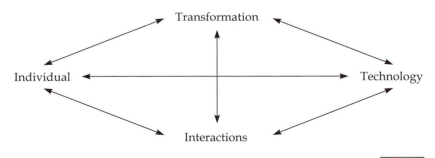

Figure 12.2
The elements of a process

problematical when questions are asked about the purpose of the business. What are the core transformations that underlie this purpose? A production director may view the engineering function as a support role to production. The engineering director may take the opposite view and that production can be subcontracted if necessary.

Central to the concept of a process is the role of the individual. The individual enables the transformation and interactions to occur, whether directly or remotely. The individual brings the qualities of being human to the transformation and interactions. The person having an off-day makes lots of mistakes, which results in the wrong deliveries being made to customers. When a person is off sick, the process is disrupted when work relating to part of the process is not done. The team comprises people who do not get on with each other, so there is no social or mechanical interaction within the team.

The individual develops views about the transformation and interactions. If the individual has a notion of what the purpose of the process is, then he may ask questions about the transformation and interactions. He may consider whether the right transformation and interactions are taking place. Are the right things being done? Attention focuses upon the acceptability or 'conduct' of what is being done. The set of transformation and interactions which relate to the movement of funds from the company bank account to a personal bank account will be acceptable if legitimate, but will be viewed as theft if not.

Usually, attention focuses upon whether what is being accomplished is acceptable. The concern is with the acceptability of the transformation's outcomes; the 'performance' of the transformation. Often performance and conduct are viewed in isolation. However, this should not be the case. Interplay exists between purpose, conduct, performance and the underlying structure. This suggests that a business's structure and strategy are mutually dependent upon each other. Each constrains or enables the other.

Finally, the role of technology must be recognized. It extends the scope of what an individual can do, both in terms of the transformation carried out and interactions enabled. The automation of processes is usually expected to improve the production of outcomes in one or more ways. The development of information technologies facilitates the collection of data and its processing and analysis. Telecommunications developments are removing location as a constraint for interactions between people. From a development perspective, the philosophical question is raised of whether the technology should be aligned to the structure or vice versa. Often the technology dictates how things will happen. Whilst technology is a great enabler, it is not a panacea in itself. The technology requires that a user, in using the technology, is trying to get some benefit from its use. Whilst the technology may run remotely for a long period of time, there will be someone who will have initiated its use.

The emerging view of a business process comprises four elements (transformation, interactions, individual and technology) and four perspectives (purpose, structure, conduct and performance). Interplay exists between each. This is illustrated in Figure 12.3.

Central is the individual. The individual, when involved in a process is engaged in purposeful activity. This purpose may be explicitly stated or tacitly implied through its actions. To achieve this purpose, certain transformations and interactions, which define the structure of the process, need to occur. The individual may enhance his ability to carry out these transformations and interactions by using technology and, in so doing, 'dehumanize' the process. When the individual assesses the process it will be in terms of its conduct and performance.

The value of this theoretical model is that it provides a useful framework to help with the practicality of mapping out existing

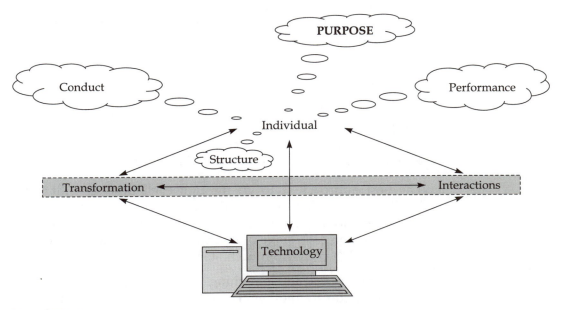

Figure 12.3 A model of a process

and new processes. Mapping processes invariably requires walking through each of the processes, collecting details en-route. The person doing the mapping will be able to identify people, bits of paper, computer screen, objects, equipment, and actual transformations and interactions. The problem is faced of how to piece all these features together to produce a useful model of the process. The solution is to interpret each feature in terms of the inputs, outcomes, transformation and interactions. Each item will have been the product of a transformation carried out by someone with a job title. That item will be transmitted somehow to another transformation carried out by someone with a job title. Whilst this task involves a lot of work, the result will be a complex map of the business processes. However, there is a simple approach that helps to overcome the complexity faced during this exercise – the 'collage'.

12.2.2 'Collage'

When trying to understand a process it is not uncommon to be overwhelmed by the perceived complexity of the process. A simple approach that is fairly effective for capturing much of this complexity is the 'collage'.

There are two prerequisites. One is the availability of wall space. Ideally the project team room (Section 11.2.1) will have this. The other is the availability of large sheets of paper, which are best hung on the walls. These sheets can be quickly and easily created from a large roll of brown paper. Three or four lengths of equal size are cut and spliced together. These sheets serve as the canvas for the collage.

The collage requires gathering samples of:

- all documentation, including title and contents pages of reports, spreadsheet printouts and templates
- screen dumps of all used computer screens
- labels, tags and any other items that informs.

The best approach is to go through each process with those involved in its day-to-day activities. Both routine and ad hoc processes should be covered. If a document is amended during a process then each stage of its amendment should be recorded, ideally with a copy from each stage.

Each item represents something that is transmitted from one transformation to another. The details to be captured for each item include who produced it, how was it produced and how often, who receives it, how is it used and how often. Gaps are to be expected in the data collected since at this stage many questions may go unanswered. However, answers will emerge at a later stage. Since these are the inputs and outputs, it is important to record the sequence in which each item arises.

The gathered items are stuck onto the prepared canvas without cluttering the canvas. The canvas is annotated as required. The aim is to map out the sequence in which these items are used. Due to the physical constrains of the canvas a number of sheets may be produced. It may be useful to have duplicate copies of each item in the event of damage to one copy.

Once the initial collage has been completed it is likely to reveal a lot of loose ends. However, every input must come from somewhere and every output should have a destination. The business process is a closed network of activities. Thus, the next task is to investigate each loose end. This will involve bringing those involved with the process together and, using the collage as a focal point for the discussion, resolving the loose ends. For example, a document may appear to stand in isolation. However, it will be generated as the outcome of an activity, which will have been triggered by an event within another process. The skill is in establishing this link. Any loose ends either have not been properly resolved or indicate redundancy. The outcome will be a set of canvasses that provide a lot of detail about all the business processes.

This technique has a number of benefits, irrespective of whether it has been used to record actual events or to design a hypothetical process.

- Since the focus is upon inputs and outputs it overcomes the methodological problem of attempting to name transformations, particularly where there are different names in use or where transformations are hidden within the confines of a piece of equipment or a computer system.
- It provides a quick and easy method to capture the complexity of a process in a way that allows the whole picture to be viewed yet maintains access to the detail of each of the parts.
- It provides a reference point for the exchange of views about issues relating to the process, which can be recorded on the 'collage'. These discussions can clear up myths held about processes. They reveal whether certain tasks are done, the meaning attached to different data fields on documents and screens, and the value of each stage.

- It provides both the foundation for establishing process documentation and an audit to verify the validity of process documentation, important from a Quality Management Systems stance.
- It provides training material.
- If kept, it provides a reference point when reviewing the process: why things were done in a certain way.

If fully exploited, the collage is a very useful approach.

12.2.3 Understand what is being done now

There is a phrase that goes along the lines of, 'If you want to go somewhere, find out where you are first.' This good advice has merit in the task ahead. By understanding what is being done now it reveals both the myths and fallacies surrounding what goes on and provides a reference point upon which to build. Despite the possibility that the redesigned process may bear no resemblance to the existing process, the value of this exercise is that it reveals the issues that need to be addressed in the redesign.

This is particularly relevant in a fast changing environment. Take the example of a small operation that is undergoing rapid growth within a company that embarks upon an implementation. At the vendor selection stage, which is when requirements are defined (Chapter 7), any attempt to understand the process will reveal what manual systems are in operation. By the time the prototyping is started, a number of months later, the impact of growth could be an increase in the number of personnel, fragmentation of work operations and the emergence of new reporting mechanisms. The requirements of new customers may have resulted in new delivery or invoicing procedures. New suppliers, selected due to the inability of existing suppliers to meet demand, may provide new opportunities for process improvement within the supply chain. However, various issues affecting the processes are still not finalized. The problem here is about how to design a process that is undergoing constant change.

At some point the process needs to be frozen. An understanding is gained about what is happening at that point and the issues that are likely to evolve or emerge are identified. During the prototyping, developments can be incorporated. The processes

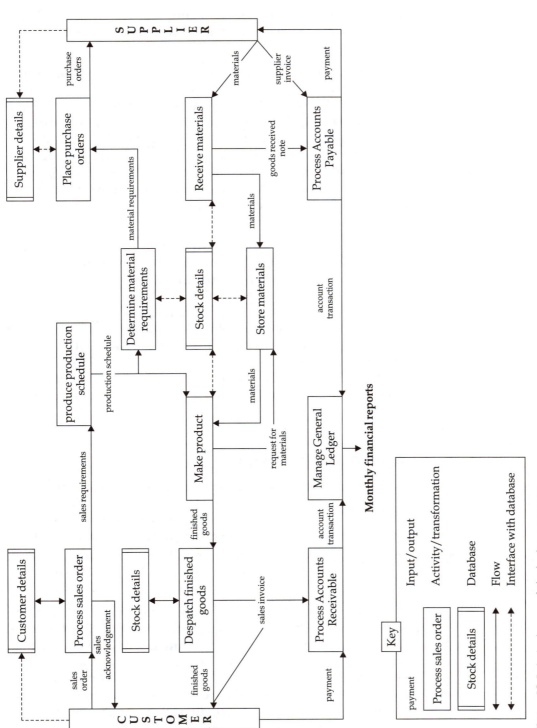

Figure 12.4 A simple map of the business process

evolve as required. By the time the GoLive is reached, the resulting processes may bear little resemblance to the initial snapshot.

The outcome of establishing what is being done will be a set of documents and diagrams. The walls of the office may be decorated with 'collages'. These present a detailed map of all the processes. If this task has been done with attention to detail, not only will the essential features of the process be captured but also details about how deviations from normal practices are handled. This map can be likened to a collection of overlapping aerial photographs laid out to present a picture of a region. Close examination will reveal all the detail, whilst standing back will reveal the dominant features.

A high-level view of what this map may look like is presented in Figure 12.4. This reveals the general flow of the business processes in terms of the principal transformations and inputs/ outputs. It also may reveal major databases, in this example those relating to customers, suppliers and stock. It does not aim to display any detail, this being the subject of other support documentation. It may reveal activities for which there is no apparent reason for doing them, legacies of a by-gone age. However, these should be treated with caution. Questions should be asked about the problems that they were trying to prevent.

12.2.4 Quick fixes

An evaluation of existing processes may reveal opportunities where small changes can make things easier. Although processes may change as a consequence of the implementation, improvements to existing processes, involving only a minimum of effort, can bring short-term gains. These 'quick fixes' may result in the cessation of unnecessary tasks or minor modifications to essential tasks.

On the other hand, the evaluation may reveal that some processes are totally inappropriate to the situation. Furthermore, a lot of effort may be required to bring about a change, which may be followed by another change as a consequence of the prototyping. The nature of the change is such that it involves re-engineering the process. When confronted with this situation, the dilemma arises about whether it is appropriate to do anything at this stage. Will the benefits offset the effort and disruption?

12.2.5 Business process re-engineering

The concept of Business Process Re-engineering made its debut in 1990 in a paper by Michael Hammer.[41] In it, he states, 'Re-engineering strives to break away from the old rules about how we organize and conduct business'. At the same time, Davenport and Short[42] were proposing that information technology could play a powerful role in the redesign of business processes. The underlying notion is that the redesign of existing practices tends not to challenge why things are done in that way. Thus, when these changes incorporate information technology the real benefits of the technology are lost.

The re-engineering approach tends to be associated with a completely fresh view of how things are done. Starting with a blank sheet, the objectives of the process are defined. Then the best way of achieving those objectives is determined. Ideas are drawn from best practices from both within and outside the particular home industry and sector. These ideas are then used to establish the new process. Whilst conceptually simple, actually doing this can be difficult.

First, management needs to have a vision of the benefits and a commitment to see the change through. Then the workforce's resistance to change needs to be overcome. Users need to buy into both the need for change and the desire for change. Finally, the change itself needs to be managed. Many of the issues are unsurprisingly not unlike those relating to the implementation of an ERP system. Indeed, the only significant difference between one and the other is the role of the ERP system as an enabler.

Thus, when confronted with the situation presented in the previous section, when a decision is required about whether to re-engineer an inappropriate process there are two options. The first is to re-engineer the process to its desired format then apply the ERP functionality. The second is to re-engineer the process within the constraints of the ERP functionality available. The argument in favour of the first approach is that it potentially provides the best solution, assuming that the software functionality is capable of doing everything required of it. This is offset by the potential for delays resulting from the development of the new process and its subsequent computerization. The later approach combines both steps, so in theory, should be quicker. However, it can be argued that best practice is being compromised to the dictates of the software.

The reality is that the benefits and lost opportunities are a function of the nature of the process and the effectiveness of making change happen. In deciding which route to adopt, each situation should be considered on its relative merits. Some processes may only be achievable through the enabling features of the ERP functionality whilst others are less dependent. For those processes that are technology enabled, it is more likely that many of the benefits of a process change may not surface with the GoLive. Rather, it is anticipated that much of the benefit will manifest within a continuous improvement environment after the GoLive. The post-GoLive period is one where the weaknesses of the design are recognized and the strengths of the system become increasingly appreciated. Whichever route is adopted, the outcome will be the definition of the process layout for the future.

12.3 Prototyping

The prototyping activity is one of the core activities of the implementation. It is this activity that establishes how things are going to be done using the new software. If necessary, processes will be re-engineered. The aim at this stage is not to produce the best way of working. Not only is this over-ambitious, but is also unlikely to occur in the short to medium term. In a dynamic environment with ongoing change to processes, it may never happen. Realistically, the process can be defined so that it adopts best practices. This is then translated into operational practice so that the processes do what is required of them. Issues that arise during the development stage are dealt with and closed off. Once live, further issues will arise. By addressing these through a continuous improvement programme (Section 14.1), the process can be improved.

During the process design activity a number of questions should be continually asked:

- What are we trying to achieve?
- What is the best way of doing this?
- Do we want to do things the way we have always done them? If so, why?
- What alternative ways are there for doing this?
- Why can I not do it the way I want to?

Answers may not be readily available, but over time, processes that are acceptable to the stakeholders should emerge. The fundamental rule regarding process design is 'keep it simple'.

During the prototyping exercise, the new process will unfold, partly under the guidance of the vendor's consultants and partly through experimentation. The more complex the process, the greater is the need to keep track of developments. A collage, generated in parallel with the process, will provide a useful diagram of the process flow highlighting loose ends and further areas for investigation. It can provide a focal point for discussion about the process, particularly with those who will be the ultimate users.

As the process unfolds, decisions are made about the numerous system settings. These settings produce the final system configuration. It is important at this stage to be careful when deciding upon particular settings since it may not be possible to change them at a later date. Some of these settings may involve fundamental business decisions such as account code structure. There is a risk being locked into a setting due to a bad decision at this design stage.

Whilst experimenting with the functionality, software bugs may arise. These need to be recorded and action taken to deal with them. It is important to ensure that these bugs are promptly resolved since progress may be hampered. There may be instances where they cannot be quickly resolved or resolved at all, in which case a work-around needs to be determined. Whilst this is not a satisfactory situation, the only alternative recourse is to escalate the matter. This action may produce the desired result but then again, if the software bug is a major technical problem it may be left unresolved.

The prototyping phase is an exciting opportunity to shape the way the business is to operate in the future. Many important decisions will be required which should involve the respective stakeholders. Many issues will be raised, some of which may require consultation with customers and suppliers. Many problems will be encountered which need to be closed. However, whether this opportunity is exploited will reflect the vision of top management, the commitment of the whole workforce and the resolve to make it happen.

12.3.1 The issues list

When problems arise, they need to be logged as an issue. The team members need to develop the discipline to log problems as they occur. Failure to do so may result in them being forgotten, to emerge at a more inconvenient time. This log provides an agenda for problem resolution. Someone is assigned to each issue that needs to be resolved and that person determines how long it should take to resolve the issue. It may be easy to resolve but for some reason it never gets addressed. Alternatively, what might be at first glance a simple objective, may be very complex in its achievement. Resolution may require the expertise of the vendor, a software modification or, in the event that a software solution cannot be found, a work-around. The list should be regularly monitored by the project manager to ensure that issues are dealt with and closed off.

12.3.2 Software modifications – compromise between process and software functionality

Orthodox thinking of those involved in ERP implementations is that modifications to the software, to provide or enhance functionality, are undesirable. The aim should be to stay 'vanilla', in other words with the unadulterated version. Apart from the cost of the modifications, upgrades are compromised and the modifications will likely require to be redone.

An alternative view is that the software should do what you want it to do.

In both cases there is a dilemma. The vanilla approach results in the software dictating how processes will function. The latter dictates functionality that the software cannot handle. Irrespective of how effective the requirements definition has been (Chapter 7), detail will have been overlooked. Alternatively, processes not thought about at that time, emerge as necessary. It is likely that there will be a mismatch between what is desired and what the software is capable of.

Hopefully, it is only with the minor details that problems arise. However, if major functionality is only cursorily examined, then there is the danger that major processes cannot function in the desired way. The resulting options are not desirable. One option is for the process to function in the way dictated by the software functionality. Alternatively, a software modification can be made, but this is likely to be expensive. If both options are disagreeable then a third solution may be to do something independent of the software, e.g. a manual system is developed or a specialized package is acquired to do the job. However, the advantage of integration is lost and other issues will arise depending upon the nature of the solution.

When resolving this, consideration should be given to the issues at play including the gap between best practice, what the system can do and what needs to be achieved. One should consider the opportunity offered by the different options. It is not uncommon for a compromise to be reached whereby a modification is decided upon. However, this should be done within the context of a controlled modification procedure. Modifications should be done only when absolutely necessary and a clear benefit is to be gained, e.g. time saved with a frequent and routine task. This procedure will address issues that include:

- nature of change
- justification for change
- who requests change and who authorizes change (two separate people)
- cost of modification
- anticipated benefit of modification
- timescale for carrying out the modification.

Modifications should be justified. If modifications are not controlled, they may occur as a result of someone's whim and result in their proliferation. Associated with this will be an escalation in costs, which will only be detected after the event. Part of this should include a sign-off procedure. The sign-off authorizes the modification to take place and accepts the modification once the modification has been carried out and has been tested to ensure that it does what it is supposed to.

It should be remembered that modifications will need to be re-applied when upgrading the system and will lead to more costs.

12.3.3 Usability

It is not uncommon for household appliances such as washing machines, microwaves and video recording equipment to host a fantastic array of functions. The only problem is that many people only require a few of these functions. Furthermore, because of the complexity involved, many people have difficulty in trying to use these functions. The result is that these people are turned away from these appliances and seek out simpler alternatives.

This situation is also common to software applications. A bewildering amount of functionality is offered on the desktop computer, but very little of it is ever used. An ERP application will have, because of its complexity, a correspondingly high amount of functionality. The presentation of this functionality will vary considerably in user friendliness from one vendor application to another.

The general user will tend to use only a limited amount of that functionality. This is aside from the security issue of restricting access to certain functionality, e.g. accounts. Thus, it is advantageous to tailor the menus and screens so that they do not deter the user, yet prevent access to restricted areas. However, this needs to be done in an economical manner as this task is time-consuming and there may be a large number of users. One approach is to organize users into groups and establish the menu structure for each group. At the screen level, where multiple screens are used in a frequent and routine manner, a single screen may be designed. As well as meeting security requirements, it can enhance user uptake. However, this needs to be done with the appreciation that processes may change in the future.

12.4 Pilot

The pilot provides an opportunity to test the final prerelease version of the process in as close to a live situation as can be simulated. It is simulation of real world events. The aim is to test the integrity of the process and expose any weaknesses prior to release. It provides an opportunity to deal with any issues so that they do not become problems when live.

12.4.1 Preparation

Preparation is essential to the success of the trial. Those involved will include many if not all the project team members and any end users whose knowledge about the working environment can contribute to the development of the simulation script. The script itself will commence with a normal transaction. The effect of this transaction upon other processes will be examined to ensure that the impact is that expected. Then deviations to the normal functioning of the process are tested.

An example is the raising of a Purchase Order (PO) against a Material Requirements Planning (MRP). Once the PO has been raised, its effect on the Open Purchase order report and any related reports can be verified. When the goods are received, the goods are booked in: the Goods Received Note (GRN) will have its details entered on the system and be logged against a PO; the stock will be allocated a stock location, perhaps in an inspection area if the part is flagged as 'to be inspected'. The impact on the stock records, MRP and Accounts Payable (AP) should be examined. Goods inspection can perform a variety of simulations at this stage to examine the effects of releasing some of the stock into stores, returning some of the stock to the supplier and placing some of the stock into quarantine so that the Material Review Board can make a decision about what to do with the stock. Again, the impact on both the stock records, MRP and AP should be examined. When the supplier invoice is received it needs to be checked against the GRN and the PO, entered onto the system, then posted to the General Ledger. Similar checks should be carried out when the supplier is paid. Problems associated with each of these stages should be identified and built into the simulation script. For example, what happens if the quantity delivered is less than that on the PO for delivery? How does one handle the incorrect matching of PO and GRN? If foreign currencies are an issue then the scenarios should include the raising of POs and supplier payments in the involved currencies, paying particular attention to the manner in which currency exchange is handled within the accounting records.

This example illustrates that a simple process can have a lot of complexity attached to it. This complexity is magnified when deviations from normal practices occur. The aim is to ensure that there is a response for handling such deviations. This means that all such deviations should be identified, ideally during the prototyping stage and built into the script as part of the simulation. This will likely require the involvement of users familiar with the day-to-day issue. The outcome is that when the process is piloted, there is a response available for dealing with each deviation. Furthermore, the impact of the response elsewhere on the system is deemed acceptable. If the testing reveals problems with the process then it presents the opportunity to develop suitable responses without being in a live situation.

Particular attention should be paid to any tasks that have involved software modifications. Does the modification do what it is supposed to do? More importantly, does it affect those other parts of the system in the way it should?

The quality of the pilot will be affected by the quality of the data available to test the processes with. Part of the preparation will include ensuring that there is adequate data on the system, identifying gaps and entering data to fill these gaps. It should be noted that a dataset that has errors in it, which will occur each time someone enters an invalid entry, may undermine the effectiveness of the pilot. Errors may confuse the interpretation of numbers. Thus, the dataset is one that is specially prepared for the pilot.

A third task, for the project manager, is to develop the pilot programme. This will summarize the sequence of the scripts, when they will run and provide an estimate of how long they will take. It will identify who is involved in the running of each script and ensure that both the people and the facilities are available when required.

The preparation is complete when the scripts are prepared, the data is ready and the programme of events is established. It is now time to carry out the pilot.

12.4.2 Simulation

The simulation ideally should take place in a room with a number of networked terminals so that those carrying out the pilot can work together. Everyone should have a copy of the scripts. The project manager can take the role of co-ordinating the simulation, ensuring that it progresses without too much delay and that problems or issues are logged. It is important that all issues are logged so that nothing is overlooked. The resultant issues list (Section 12.3.1) provides an agenda for the follow-up.

Time needs to be available so that all the required checks can be made. Movement from one step to the next should only be done when all the required checks have been carried out for that step. In this way, the impact of one step cannot be confused with a number of steps as would be the case if a check was only carried out every, say, ten steps. The effect is that the pilot may be slow. However, it should be remembered that this is the ideal time to test whether the system does what it should be doing.

If the testing reveals problems with the process then it presents the opportunity to develop suitable responses without being in a live situation.

One opportunity the pilot provides is the possibility for the system administrator to get an initial glimpse of how running the software affects system performance, e.g. disk space, effect on other applications, network traffic. Whilst this may be only a token insight, it may be sufficient to reveal whether there are any technological hitches.

12.4.3 Follow-up

The follow-up to the actual simulation is the resolution of any issues that arise. The issues list (Section 12.3.1) created provides an agenda for further action. Once issues have been dealt with then the pilot should be repeated. This cycle of piloting, identifying issues, resolving them, then piloting continues until all issues are resolved. When everyone is satisfied that the process functions as required, it may be desirable to get the project manager, the project team and the ultimate process owners to sign off that the process is acceptable. This can avoid post-live finger pointing when things go wrong.

12.5 Responsibilities

The quickest way to expose company politics is to fail to assign responsibilities for all tasks. If a task is highlighted after GoLive yet no one is assigned responsibility for doing it, the outcome can degenerate into squabbling about who should have responsibility for the task. Furthermore, once responsibility is assigned, the appropriate documentation will need to be updated to record this. Whilst the more routine processes will be clearly assigned, the danger arises of overlooking less routine processes, such as month end tasks. More easily overlooked are responsibilities for data set-up. If there is a new supplier to be added to the system, who has responsibility for setting up all the parameters, not forgetting bank details so that the supplier can be paid? In this case, responsibility for different parameters may be divided between purchasing and accounts; purchasing having responsibility for all details barring those relating to the bank and payment terms, which are assigned to accounts.

A prudent task is to compile two lists. The first list identifies all distinct processes. The second list identifies all distinct data set-up categories, e.g. supplier details, routings, price lists, chart of accounts updates. For both lists, the roles involved need to be identified, responsibilities assigned and agreed. It should be noted that the people involved in collecting data for entry may be different from those that enter the data onto the system. Assigning responsibilities is perhaps best done before the processes are finalized, as it ensures that those assigned responsibility for the task have the opportunity to become involved in the final phase of the process development.

12.6 Documentation

Documentation is the final stage of the process development. Documentation includes all procedures, instructions and templates related to the process. Procedures and instructions inform people how they should be doing things. Procedures and instructions must thus reflect what is done. Templates may be required for recording data that is not collectable via the computer. Documentation also includes job descriptions, since work may have been redefined following process re-engineering. Not to be overlooked are reports and stationery. Whilst altruistic ambitions of the paperless office might be a pervading philosophy, the reality is that documents are essential.

If the organization adheres to an international standard for its Quality Management System, e.g. the ISO 9000 series, then there will be a requirement for appropriate documentation. If redefined processes do not have supporting documentation then the organization is in breach of the quality standard.

Documentation related to procedures, irrespective of whether it is related to the Quality Management System, should fall within the document control procedure. This should require a standard documentation format and procedures for the authorization, issue, change and withdrawal of documents. When a process changes, its documentation will change in a controlled manner. If the documentation is not available, then the undocumented process is not compliant with the philosophy and practice of all processes being documented. One route around this is to get authorization from the process control administrator to run the process under a 'concession'. However, this evasive action impedes the provision of training materials. The documentation provides basic material for training people on the processes, so should be available at the time of training.

12.6.1 Procedures and work instructions

Procedures and work instructions describe how tasks are carried out, the latter in more detail. The production of these documents is not a task for one person, but for those who define the processes. The process of producing this documentation commences during the prototyping and develops through the piloting, at the end of which it is finalized. A useful approach to adopt is to take a sequence of screen dumps of the required screens and paste them in a Microsoft Word or equivalent document. This document then can be edited as required and provides the basis for future documents. Where appropriate, the application manuals or on-line help files should be used, though where the language used is unclear, this material should be translated into a meaningful form.

As a wide range of processes is likely to be affected, this is an opportunity to review the format of the organization's documentation. Document headings are likely to include:

- process name
- purpose of process
- description of process
- roles responsible for process operation and maintenance
- process flow
- detailed instructions
- details of related documentation.

Each document should have an issue number, author and date created.

The project manager may find it useful to generate a list of all the documentation and use this list to monitor its completion. If a list of processes has been generated for the assignment of responsibilities (Section 12.5) then this list can be used to identify the relevant documentation requirements. Documentation should not be left to the last minute as there is a danger that it will not be available for the training or more importantly for the GoLive.

12.6.2 Job descriptions

The development of new processes will result in the emergence of new job descriptions. Automation of manual tasks and the creation of new tasks make this inevitable. However, people tend to be resistant to change. Thus, human resource personnel need to be involved at an early stage in the implementation. The implications relating to changes in job descriptions need to be handled in an agreeable and friendly manner. Unions need to be kept informed. Throughout, the benefits of what is being pursued should be promoted as well as the well being of those affected. In organizations where change is a pervasive feature of life this should not be a problem. In organizations where change is unknown then this has the potential to become a big issue. Handled carefully, everyone should emerge smiling.

12.6.3 Reports

Whereas procedures inform people about how to enter data onto the system, that data should be used to inform people about what is happening. This can be done in a number of ways. Specific information can be accessed using the data entry screen, though with care, to avoid accidental data entry, deletion or change. Alternatively, the standard off-the-shelf reports provided with the application can be displayed on the monitor screen, downloaded in a softcopy format for further processing in, for example, a spreadsheet, or printed in a hardcopy format – the paper report. One task for the project team is to identify the reports available, then make the users, including managers, aware of what is available and where they can find the report.

If standard reports fail to give the information required, alternatives should be examined. For ad hoc queries, a query tool, perhaps provided with the application, enables access to the data. However, as raised in Section 3.1, this should be used with caution by those unfamiliar with its pitfalls. Business Intelligence tools support more sophisticated analysis of the data but tend to be third party applications, which may not have been purchased, and which involve technical expertise in their set up. In both cases, users will require a high level of technical training to become competent in the use of these approaches. This will also take time.

Another approach is to develop reports tailored to suit requirements. Whilst this will have a training requirement, in the short term, it may be a relatively quick means for meeting information requirements. A limited number of people are selected to develop report-writing skills. These are likely to include the systems administrator and selected team members. Note that if only one person learns these skills, then this could become a bottleneck if the demand for reports is great, or that person is absent for some reason.

Consideration needs to be given to when these reports are to be generated. If these reports are generated during the implementation phase, then they are designed to meet anticipated requirements. However, these requirements may change once the transfer is made into the live situation and the requirements are better understood. This will create additional work, involving the rework or perhaps complete redesign of the reports. Alternatively, requirements can wait until after the GoLive. In this case, users may develop a better appreciation of their requirements from their experiences, with the result of a better report specification. However, this has the disadvantage of delaying access to the informative value of the system. It is likely that a compromise will be reached whereby some reports are generated during the implementation whilst others emerge after the GoLive.

The actual process of generating a customized report should follow a controlled procedure, co-ordinated by the project manager. A request should be accompanied by a specification. This specification should contain information about the requester, the purpose of the report, column headings, selection criteria, sort criteria and any special requirements such as calculations. The report writers will assesss whether they are able to produce the report or whether it will require vendor technical support. When external support is required, quotes and estimates of timescale are required so that the merits of the additional expenditure are evaluated. It may be possible to find an alternative solution to resolving specific information requirements. The value of having a controlled procedure is that it ensures that reports are produced within a reasonable time. It also reduces the opportunity for creep to arise, whereby reports are continually changing, because the end user cannot make up his mind about what he wants.

12.6.4 Stationery

It is assumed that the documentation sent to customers and suppliers uses preprinted stationery. This documentation presents an image of the company. Furthermore, the preprinted stationery may be expensive and the technology used to print the documentation may be dated. The implementation provides an opportunity to review both this image and the means to produce the documentation. There are two options (Section 3.1), continue to use preprinted stationery and dedicated printers or print documents as required using the stationery format embedded in the print command. There may be an opportunity for cost savings by eliminating the need for preprinted stationery. If the decision is taken to use preprinted stationery then the task may be simply one of configuring the printers to handle the data from the new application. However, configuring the printers may not be technologically possible, raising the question of what to do: design new preprinted stationery that can be used? Purchase new printers? Alternatively, it may be decided to use documents that are formatted at the time of print.

Whichever route is adopted, it is necessary to identify all the required documents. A list might include some or all of the following:

- sales orders
- sales order acknowledgements
- sales invoice
- delivery notes
- credits
- debits
- purchase orders
- customer statements
- bar-coded labels.

If the documents are being redesigned, preprinted or otherwise, the requirements need to be established for each document type. Attention to detail is essential. As well as establishing the design layout, many questions can be asked about what goes in each document:

- Is there a logo?
- Is colouring an issue?
- What are the data fields and how do these map to the system data fields?
- What information is mandatory, e.g. company registration number?
- What additional information should be displayed that might be useful, such as contact names, direct telephone numbers and name of the person who created the document (when in use)?
- What headings are required?
- What are the units of measurement and how are these to be displayed?
- How are foreign currencies and languages to be handled?
- What additional annotation is required?
- How are terms and conditions to be handled?

Decisions may require the involvement of a number of people, who should be involved during the whole process. As with any design process, no sooner has one format been decided than someone decides to change something. This needs to be controlled since changes can delay and frustrate. Each document should have ownership assigned to someone. They should sign off the final version to indicate that they accept it. This implies that they have checked it thoroughly before it is released. If errors are found after its release, they can be expensive to correct. What do you do with preprinted stationery with an error in it? How quickly can you get a programmer to change the error if it is in an embedded format? Perhaps close to the hearts of accountants is the question of whose budget any additional costs come out off.

If the stationery format is to be embedded so that it is printed at the time the document is produced then the question arises about how this documentation is to be developed. There are a number of issues to consider. The tools to produce these documents may require a level of skill beyond that available in-house. It may be questioned whether it is cost effective to develop the skills in-house. It will take time to train someone. Once the initial set of documents have been produced, changes may be so infrequent that it is possible and cost effective to depend upon external support. However, what is the nature of this external support? Whilst the tool is likely to be third party, can the vendor provide adequate support? How quickly can someone be available to make changes when required or deal with problems when they occur? There could be a two-month wait before a programmer is free. It is possible that the development work be done remotely via modem link. If this is the case, then time will be tied up in trying to explain things over the telephone. As with any aspect of the ERP implementation, the events should be planned and project managed so that documentation is available when required.

12.7 Implementation of the training strategy – phase 2

This phase in the training is the end user and manager training. The aim is to disseminate throughout the organization the project team's knowledge and skills relating to the application and the new processes. The expected outcome is the trainees being able to use the system.

12.7.1 The programme

For this phase, a programme can be developed which covers all the areas required. It can be organized into different themes to reflect different topics and audiences. Whilst a general overview will appeal to everyone, the specialist areas will only be relevant to a limited number of people.

One topic, which will be relevant to everyone, is log in and user security. Not to be overlooked is the fact that there may be new users who have no keyboard skills. Thus, a basic keyboard skills course should be contemplated.

Two audiences can be distinguished: end users and managers. Whilst the former will be interested in how to use the system, the managers will be more interested in how to get information about the system. The users can be further differentiated into casual users, normal users and reflective users. The interest of casual users is limited to being able to perform certain tasks when required of them. Normal users are regular users of a specific suite of functions. Their main interest is using the system to do their job. Reflective users will want a deeper understanding of how the system works so that they can solve problems and make improvements. Thus, it may be appropriate to distinguish two levels of training: that essential to carry out tasks and a more detailed session on the finer points of the system.

The format of this training will tend to be structured into formal training workshops based around a PC. The data should ideally be that which they will be using when live so that real-life situations can be simulated. This may require data set-up preparation. Whilst the training material should be task orientated, it will be explanatory in order to encourage an appreciation of why things are done in the way that they are. The project team room can be made available for trainees to practice on their own as a follow-up to the training courses.

The trainers will be the new 'experts' on the system, the project team members. Phase 1 training should have included training for the team in how to train.

The timing of the training should be such that there is not a long gap between receiving training and using the application. A refresher course may need to be considered as a contingency.

The cost of the training should be monitored against budget.

12.7.2 Plan

At the detailed level of each individual session, its preparation will be underpinned by its plan, which will deal with:

- objectives
- trainer
- audience
- time
- location
- facilities
- content and content structure

- method
- resources/materials
- cost.

Many of the issues have already been covered in Section 11.4.3. A simple template (Figure 12.5) provides an aid to reduce the likelihood that something is overlooked.

Training plan

General information
Date: Location:
Topic: Duration:
Aim: Audience:

Objectives:

Introduction

Duration	Key content	Method	Resources	Assessment

Body

Duration	Key content	Method	Resources	Assessment

Conclusion

Duration	Key content	Method	Resources	Assessment

Review

Figure 12.5
A training plan template

12.7.3 Deliver and assess

Delivery of the training is complemented by an assessment to ensure that the delivery has been successful.

During the delivery, the trainer will be confronted by a mixture of attitudes and expectations. Whilst there will be those with a positive outlook, there will be others who have a negative view about the situation. Likewise, some may have high expectations about the quality of training and fail to appreciate the inexperience of the trainers. Thus, the trainers need to be aware that they may not be well received and be able to respond accordingly. This highlights the importance of the trainers being trained in the training process.

The delivery of the training should result in the trainees developing the requisite skills being taught. To ensure that this is being done, some form of assessment should be carried out. Already raised in Section 11.4.5, the emphasis is upon assessing what level of skill or knowledge has been attained. However, it should be remembered that the trainees are less likely to retain this knowledge or skill the longer the time that passes before they are required to use it. Thus, the assessment may only reveal what the person is capable to attaining rather than providing an indication that the person is competent at a specific task. It may be necessary to provide refresher courses closer to the GoLive.

12.7.4 Review

After each session has been completed, it should be reviewed in order to reflect upon the problems, and assess what worked and what could have been done better. The issues raised may be concerned with the material being presented and highlight the need for its revision. Alternatively, it may highlight issues with people and the need to establish a strategy for handling them. Each situation will be different, but each will contribute to an accumulating wealth of experience that, when continuously fed into subsequent training sessions, should make these sessions more successful learning experiences for the trainees.

12.8 Data set up

Data are the basis for all events within the business. Data is everywhere, whether stored on hard disk, chalked on black-boards or scribbled on paper. Its value is to inform. If it is not correct then we are not correctly informed and then we make decisions that are wrong. From these decisions are actions that are not appropriate to the situation. The outcome? Time and effort to put things right; perhaps lost customers, disgruntled employees and distrustful suppliers. And there will be a cost element too.

The opportunity exists to ensure that the data for the new application is clean, in other words, error free. How important this is will reflect attitudes towards data accuracy. Some people will accept that the data is full of errors and live with it. It does not matter to them and if mistakes occur then it is just one of those things. Some will argue that having gone through the process of cleaning the data up, errors are introduced by users when the system is live, so why bother?

The key issue is that the integrity of the system is compromised with data errors, whether at set-up or when in on-going use. This affects the effectiveness of the information system to function as required. Furthermore, as integration is a character-istic of an ERP system, errors are transferred; perhaps passing unnoticed until an event arises which exposes them, e.g. accounting month end. Data errors reduce confidence in the system and can lead to the emergence of practices such as the use of a spreadsheet with the same data 'because it is more accurate'. The ability of suppliers and customers to gain limited access to your database exposes the issue of their confidence in the data that they see. Thus, not only is it desirable to have clean data when the system goes live, practices should be such that the data remains clean during on-going use. However, the first task is to get the data onto the system.

12.8.1 Migration of data

There are two basic ways of getting data onto the system. Data can be manually typed in or can be electronically transferred. The former is obviously slower being labour intensive and more costly. Although the data can be checked for errors prior to entry, there is no guarantee that the manual input is error free. The electronic transfer is in principle faster and cleaner, particularly for large amounts of data. However, there are various considera-tions. First is the assumption that the data can be produced on the old system in a format that is accessible. Second, having accessed the data, additional data may be required before it can be accepted by the new system. This may occur where there are additional data fields, such as flags, to those downloaded. Alternatively, the data may require conversion or reformatting.

The time for cleaning the data may be at the intermediary stage after the data has been downloaded from the old system and prior to upload on to the new system. The electronic input is likely to require the technical expertise of the software vendor.

Data migration is a complex process. Whichever approach is adopted, although it is likely that both modes will be involved, the migration of data onto the new system will need planning in detail and at an early enough point in the implementation to ensure that this process is completed on time. Questions that need to be addressed include:

- What data is required on the new system?
- Can this data be transferred from the old system?
- What data is required that is not on the old system?
- Does this data exist elsewhere and how can it be best input?
- How will the data be cleaned?
- What (static) data can be transferred prior to going live and what (dynamic) data can only be transferred after the last use of the old system?
- Who will check the data and when?
- Who will input the data and when?
- How will the data entry process be managed?
- How will the accuracy of the data entered be verified?

Static data can be entered over a period of time. The dynamic data, data that changes over time can only be transferred after the last transaction on the old system. Examples of dynamic data include purchase orders, sales orders and stock details. The migration of the dynamic data may require several days, so it is not uncommon to plan the GoLive date to coincide with a long weekend. This provides more time to ensure that the data migration is completed and reduces the likelihood of lost working days due to the absence of an information system.

12.9 Last minute check

The time has arrived, the users have been trained, the processes tested, the documentation distributed and the data set up on the system. The hardware has been checked and the printers are functional. What has been overlooked? It is worth asking this question because it can just as likely be a minor detail and something obvious that no-one has thought about. This is an open question and anyone is welcome to respond to it.

GoLive/review

Ideally, when the new system goes live, people switch from their old practices to those required by the new system. If everyone is properly trained, then each person will know what he or she has to do on the GoLive day. If the processes have been properly tested then operations will progress smoothly. If the data migration has been properly handled then the data will make sense to those using it. The success of the GoLive day is measured by the lack of problems. The overwhelming feeling of anticlimax undermines the achievement of one of the most significant milestones in the implementation. However, the implementation is not finished. Work then begins on realizing the benefits of the new system.

However, if problems are experienced on and after GoLive, mechanisms need to be in-place to deal with them.

13.1 Problems and problem resolution

When problems arise there should be a problem response mechanism which deals with them and which everyone is aware of. This mechanism should be simple and provide a means for tracking progress in resolving the problem. When a problem is identified, it should be reported to the person assigned with responsibility for co-ordinating problem resolution. This may be the project manager.

Initial investigation will reveal whether the problem is readily resolved, requires further investigation or whether it is something that needs to be transferred to the vendor to deal with. Details about the problem are required. This will include a description of what was being done at the time the problem arose. Evidence should be collected about the problem in the form of screen dumps and any relevant documentation.

The problem co-ordinator will establish who is going to deal with the problem and keep track of progress in resolving the problem. Readily resolved problems can be closed off quickly. The rest need to be monitored to ensure that they are being addressed. This is particularly important for problems that affect critical tasks, for example those relating to month-end activities. When a problem is referred to the vendor, this tends to be through the vendor's user help-desk.

13.1.1 The user help-desk

The user help-desk is a call centre facility provided by the vendor, which allows the client to log problems that he cannot resolve. The hours of access tend to be normal office hours, although this will vary according to vendor.

A typical cycle of events is as follows. When a problem is logged all the available information about the problem is reported and its urgency is highlighted. The vendor assigns the problem a unique identification number and gives an indication of when someone will be able to look at it. At some point, a programmer will seek permission to dial into the system and, if given, will dial in to investigate the problem. If the programmer can fix the problem then this will be done. Otherwise, it will be investigated further. In the cases where further investigation is required, the client should monitor progress to ensure that the problem is being addressed. It may be eventually admitted that the problem cannot be fixed. If the problem was an isolated event then it may not be cause for concern. However, repeat occurrences will require a work-around solution. Whilst this is inconvenient, it provides a means to bypass the problem while discussions ensue with the vendor about how they will deal with it. Over time, most problems raised will be closed off. Those problems that are not resolved need to be taken up directly with the vendor.

Whilst this service will be part of the maintenance agreement there is a distinction between technical problems and those caused by user carelessness. The latter, if recurring, may incur a charge.

From a problem co-ordination viewpoint, it is practical that the client has only designated people who access the user help-desk.

Thus, when problems are reported, they are logged alongside the other problems. The key point is that all problems, irrespective of who is resolving them, need to be logged and monitored to ensure that they are resolved in an acceptable and timely manner and closed off.

13.1.2 The first month end

The month end process should follow a clearly defined procedure in which all tasks are listed and those responsible for doing them are identified.

The first month end is a potentially nail-biting period as it may reveal problems, which, because of their nature, have remained hidden from view. Operational problems surface as they occur. However, with an integrated system, operational issues are translated into accounting numbers. Anomalous values may be picked up in the course of day-to-day business, but, unless you are looking for these numbers, they pass unnoticed. It may be possible to run off trial balances at regular intervals during this first period to glean any irregularities. This provides an opportunity to catch the more apparent problems. However, the first comprehensive picture of whether the accounting numbers balance and make sense will arise during the month end process. Examination of these numbers will reveal anomalies and so, prompt investigation. Incorrect account code set up or missing account codes may be the reason.

Similarly, the year end process will have its own procedure. However, if the month end processes have been problem free then, from an implementation perspective, the year end process can be expected to be problem free. Nevertheless, the unexpected can arise at any time.

13.2 Review

At some point following the GoLive, it is useful to reflect upon the implementation and consider how the implementation progressed. Six weeks is an appropriate period as it allows the system to bed down and also permits an accounting month end to have taken place.

The review provides an opportunity to learn from the implementation:

- Does the software do what is expected of it? What are the outstanding or emergent issues?

- What can be learnt from the implementation? What could have been done better? How can this be used in future?
- What timescale/budget is required to deal with the remaining issues?
- Has the project been a success (see Section 11.2.7 for a brief discussion about what constitutes success)?

This is particularly invaluable if there are successive phases involving the introduction of additional functionality. It should include eliciting feedback from users and managers. This feedback may reveal issues that can be readily addressed such as the provision of extra training.

This review is not the end of the implementation, merely a transition event marking the shift into the next major phase of the ERP implementation cycle.

14

On-going

The implementation should never really stop. The benefits anticipated at the outset may not arise without further attention to the processes, as the prototyping process is unlikely to yield optimum solutions. Once a particular process has gone live and has had time to settle down, issues emerge which, if dealt with, can lead to the improvement of the processes. Furthermore, it is worth remembering that the ERP system is merely a tool to facilitate activities within the business. Thus, when improvements occur they need not be directly concerned with the ERP system. Improvements in the use of the ERP system are an outcome of improvements in the process. These improvements can take place informally as the need arises or in an environment in which improvements are part of the culture. Where improvements are part of the culture, they tend to take place within a framework, under a banner of say Total Quality Management or Continuous Improvement Programme). Furthermore, a key aspect of the culture can be described by an expression that has emerged in the 1990s – The Learning Organization. Together, they provide a means for maintaining change as a strategic weapon for establishing and maintaining competitive edge.

When the point in time is reached where the tool – the ERP system – is viewed more as a hindrance than an enabler, then the implementation cycle completes the circle. The question that is asked is whether to upgrade or replace with a new system. Whichever the decision, the outcome is to start the cycle again.

This chapter will provide a brief introduction to some of the broader issues relating to improvement then close the cycle by looking at some of the issues relating to the debate about upgrade or replacement.

14.1 Continuous improvement

Continuous improvement has been the subject of much interest, particularly during the 1980s when it first rose to prominence. The underlying principle is that there is a continuing search for better ways of doing things. When adopted as a company philosophy, it involves everyone. The approach tends to be organized around a company-wide programme of activities. This programme often takes place under the banner of Total Quality and is regarded as the domain of quality.

The features of a Continuous Improvement Programme are presented in Table 14.1. There are strong similarities with an ERP implementation, which is perhaps not unsurprising, as the focus of both is upon the management of change. The differences are more revealing. The ERP implementation tends to be project focused, with a beginning and an end. Continuous improvement is part of the day-to-day work activity for which time is made available. The team approach within ERP tends to be primarily orientated around the project team. This reflects the fact that much of the work is carried out by individuals who work in consultation with others. Continuous improvement teams form to deal with a specific issue or set of issues, then disband when that issue has been dealt with. Alternatively, the team may have a process focus, whereby they are looking at a specific process and ways that it can be improved. At any one time there are numerous teams, whose membership is comprised of those with an immediate interest in the topic. It may well be that everyone belongs to at least one team.

One approach to continuous improvement recognizes that there are a series of stages that mark the transition from being out of control to one that is striving for excellence. At the outset the assumption is that processes are out of control.

The first step is to attain a state of control. The quality literature provides precise definitions about when a process is deemed to be in a state of control, drawing upon statistical approaches to process evaluation. A more general view is that a process can be viewed as being in a state of control when it generates acceptable outcomes. In other words, unacceptable outcomes

Table 14.1 Features of a Continuous Improvement Programme

Objective	To become more competitive To lower costs To improve customer satisfaction

Approach	By means of a company-wide continuous improvement programme, to reduce non-conformance in all activities. This requires:
	
	• understanding of the business, the process making up the business and the implications of the change
	• focus
	employing
	  • planning, implementation and control
	  • education/training of the workforce, including management

Participants	All people within the organization, requiring • individual understanding and awareness (by effective communication) and responsibility (for action) • recognition for success • management commitment and leadership . . . especially from top management

Notes

1 A clear understanding of the processes is required.
2 Ownership for all processes needs to be established.
3 The organization for continuous improvement tends to comprise of a Steering Committee and teams (Quality Circles, Task Forces). The Steering Committee handles strategic issues, whilst the teams handle operational issues.
4 Performance measures (Critical Success Factors, Key Performance Indices, Statistical Process Control) are required to monitor progress.
5 Recognition is essential though this need not be financially based. The aim is to have people working together rather than competing against each other.

are infrequent. A simple approach to establishing control is to identify the problems and systematically work at eliminating them. When the production of unacceptable outcomes has been reduced to an infrequent occurrence then the process can be described loosely as controlled.

The next stage is to move towards a state of improvement. Attention now focuses upon how to produce acceptable outcomes more efficiently. Are there better ways for doing things? It might be expected that the implementation would have established the best way of doing things. On the contrary, the implementation will have identified and implemented a better way of doing things. However, in extreme cases, it may not be the best way of doing things. For various reasons it may have been decided that a transition to a completely different approach was inappropriate at this stage and left to this later date. One such example is the move to a kanban system. In this hypothetical example, it may be thought that a continuous improvement environment, with user involvement through improvement teams, would be more conducive to success than an implementation environment. In general, the template for best practice is likely to have been laid down during the implementation prototyping. It is through time-tested use of the new practices that weaknesses are recognized and opportunities sensed, investigated and developed.

The third stage is to move towards a state of excellence. The focus is upon best practice and the approach adopted tends to be benchmarking. Benchmarking is the searching out of best practices and incorporation of those transferable elements of best practice to one's own processes. These practices may be found internally elsewhere within the organization, in competitor companies or in completely different industries. As the search becomes more extensive, the opportunities for completely fresh insight magnify. This approach offers the opportunity of significant improvements and optimal levels of performance. In doing so, the process moves from a state of improvement to a state of excellence. However, to the unwary, there is the danger of adopting 'best practices' that are inappropriate to the business.

This three-stage process provides a simple framework to guide the continuous improvement effort. It may be appropriate to collapse the second and third stages by adopting a benchmarking approach as a means for improving the process. To ignore the first stage may result in failure to understand why unacceptable outcomes are occurring. This has the impact that those features, which give rise to unacceptable outcomes, are transferred.

Continuous improvement is the logical extension of the implementation project. It enables the rough practices that were developed in the artificial situation of the project team environment to be refined and tuned within the reality of day-to-day operations by those who are in the best position to effect the change: those doing the work. As a company-wide practice, it can be inaugurated at any time, though it does require organization, commitment and planning. The transition from the project team to the continuous improvement team should be planned in advance. The outcome of continuous improvement is the transition from the potential to realize the benefits (Section 6.3) of the ERP application to the likelihood that these benefits are realized.

This brief introduction to the subject of continuous improvement is expanded in the many books that are available on the subject. A selection is provided in the Selected reading list at the end of this book. Whilst the conditions necessary for continuous improvement tend to be as described here, individual practices differ. Those that are successful are those that have managed to knit a good fit with the organizational culture.

14.1.1 The cultural dimension

Articles on subjects related to organizational change often make reference to the nebulous term 'culture'. It can be appreciated that a culture where everyone works together is likely to effect change more successively than one that is characterized by infighting. The message is that some cultures are more conducive to change than others. Underpinning this message is the notion that there is *something* particular to the group of people that constitute the organization. This *something* is not visible but can have an important influence upon how the group of people function together. This *something* or culture has attracted much debate. One useful definition describes culture as 'the shared philosophies, ideologies, values, assumptions, beliefs, expectations, attitudes, and norms that knit a community together' (Kilman *et al.*, 1986).[43]. Paraphrased, 'this is the way we do things here'.

However, as revealed by Edgar Schein,[44] a culture does not stand still: it evolves over time. The departure of long-serving employees, new recruits, more demanding customers or legislative requirements are some of the influences which can modify the prevailing culture. If a culture can change then the question arises whether a culture can be shaped to a more desirable state. What can be done to change a culture? Make it more conducive to change. This has attracted much debate, particularly in the context of continuous improvement and Total Quality Management. However, there appear to be no easy answers.

Successful efforts to affect a culture involve a variety of activities. Top management promote a vision of how they would like things to happen. This is backed up by events that reinforce the message. The focus is upon the entire workforce. Events can take many guises. They deal with both the symbolism associated with practices as well as practices themselves. This symbolism is illustrated in a few examples: consider the meaning conveyed by management car-park allocations, open-plan offices, good housekeeping discipline, poor reward/pay systems or uniforms. Those symbols that are at odds with the vision are removed or replaced with symbols that are in-line with the vision. Care must be taken to ensure that events are in line with the message. The company that espouses a no-blame culture but engages in witch-hunts to find out who is responsible for misdemeanours is unlikely to be taken seriously by its workforce. Culture change can be fraught with problems. Well-entrenched habits can be difficult to change. Long established traditions can resist efforts to abandon. Unintended and undesirable side effects may result. Good intentions can lead to bad feelings among those affected. Cultural change can be difficult to make happen. There does not appear to be a formula for effecting cultural change. Instead, cultural change appears to be an almost invisible gradual process involving a combination of events that act in a manner unique to that particular organization.

This concept of culture is an important issue that should be both appreciated and addressed. From an ERP perspective, a culture that embraces change is desirable for a successful implementation. It forms part of the conditions conducive for change. Nevertheless, it can be argued that a project management approach to an ERP implementation, supported by a strong senior management, can force through the implementation. New practices can be imposed upon the workforce. However, these practices will be mechanically carried out and the impetus for doing things better will be absent. The continuous improvement phase of the implementation is highly unlikely to happen. Once the system is up and running, things return to 'normal'.

14.1.2 Organizational learning and the learning organization

For most people involved in an ERP implementation, the whole cycle is a learning experience. The project team members are gaining new knowledge. The end users are learning new skills. The managers are learning new approaches for understanding what is happening. The fact that so many people within the organization are involved raises the notion of communal learning, more commonly referred to as organizational learning.

Despite its recent widespread use, the concept of organizational learning is not new. Shrivastava[45] produced a review in 1983 revealing that many different theories existed about organizational learning. In it, he highlights the necessity of organizational learning 'for the formulation of organizational strategies and broader organizational changes'. He distinguishes between an individual's learning and the participation of individuals in the sharing of knowledge and expertise. Systems to support learning range from informal networks to formal mechanisms. Whilst some systems emerge, others are designed. The most formal mechanisms are regulation-bound bureaucracies.

A review in 1997 by Easterby-Smith[46] reinforced the message that there are many different ways of considering organizational learning. Underpinning these is an attempt to understand learning processes within organizations. This is distinct from the notion of a learning organization, which Easterby-Smith describes as an idealized organization where 'learning is maximized'. The person most commonly associated with this notion is Peter Senge through his book *The Fifth Discipline*. However, efforts to create a learning organization are perhaps more aspirational rather than practical as 'the learning organization is a goal to be pursued rather than a state of affairs to be achieved'(King, 2001).[47] Whilst it may result in an ideological outlook on the role of learning within the organization, the reality may be development of systems and practices which support the capture, use and sharing of data, the development of skills, knowledge and intellectual property and the stimulation of creativity. King proposes six strategies that address aspects of these issues. The implementation of these strategies focuses upon processes or mechanisms that support learning and organizational learning, in the broadest sense of their meaning. The obvious impact is upon the culture of the organization. Learning becomes an accepted part of life.

ERP is about change and if this change is to ensue successfully then it requires the collective ability of people to understand their environment, learn about possibilities for the future and then make them happen. To this end, an organization that embarks upon an ERP implementation may benefit by considering itself as a learning organization and adopting practices relating to the different aspects of learning presented in this very cursory overview of the subject. Their adoption may in turn have an impact upon the organizational culture in such a way as to enhance the conditions conducive to a successful ERP implementation.

14.2 Upgrading versus new software

The point in time comes when the existing system is deemed to have served its purpose and is viewed more as a hindrance to progress than as an enabler. With the passage of time, a decision about what to do may be continually put off. The opportunity to seek the benefits of a new or upgraded system is offset by the distraction of the potential cost and effort. This delay may postpone the incidence of changeover costs, but this is offset by the costs incurred through missed opportunities associated with the enhanced functionality.

When the decision is finally taken to do something there are three options: upgrade, refurbish or replace. One should consider what advantage is offered by each option and how each is offset by issues such as cost, disruption, or risk of new, untested, bug-ridden software.

Upgrade has the advantage that people are familiar with both the software and the vendor. Also an upgrade may be more quickly implemented than a replacement. The vendor should have upgrade experience, so can facilitate a smooth transition. However, this is offset by whether the upgraded technology really offers any advantages. Involvement with a user group may allow the vendor to be influenced about the development path of its functionality, resulting in individual modules that meet specific requirements and provide identifiable benefits. If the gap between the existing licensed version and the latest release is great there may be significant differences in the software. The look and feel may be totally different. The underlying code may have been totally rewritten, using a 4GL rather than a 3GL. It may just not be possible to simply substitute the existing version for an upgrade and then phase in use of the additional functionality. A full implementation may be required. Interestingly this outlook may become outdated with the componentization of packages. The concept is that a required component is downloaded from the vendor's portal and 'plugged in'. Attention focuses only upon the activities relating to that component. Thus, the upgrade process is simpler and more manageable and done on a needs basis. However, the reality may be different. One component may require other components to function. Thus, the upgrade may require the downloading of a set of components and involve as much work as the traditional upgrade.

The refurbishment of the existing application involves its customization to meet the new requirements. If the application has already had a lot of investment made in its customization this may be an acceptable option. However, a variety of issues should be considered: the age of the host software, scale of the additional requirements, who has access to the code, what are the contractual issues regarding the code, who is doing the modification, how familiar are they with the code, how quickly is a solution required, how does the modification affect vendor support, is the functionality required unique to your application, . . . There are a host of issues and this exercise is likely to appeal only to the larger organizations.

Finally, there is the option to replace the legacy system with a new system with its associated challenges and opportunities.

Whichever option is decided upon, the implementation cycle has returned to its starting point. The cycle begins again with the need and how this need is to be fulfilled.

15

Finale

The great thing about books like this is that they impart knowledge, they provide food for thought and they provide an opportunity for criticism. The great thing about people is that no matter how great they are – they can get it wrong. No matter how good the company, a number of years later, it, with only a few exceptions, hits the doldrums. Management theory is full of case study examples of what is right, but the company that is subject to the case study examination usually undoes its cause by doing something that brings about a crisis.

The problem with books like this is that they do not provide answers to all the problems that arise. But what book can?

This book is about both theory and real life experiences. There are many issues involved in an implementation. What is right in one situation may be wrong in another. The issue is less about following a set of rules and more about being aware of what is going on and behaving accordingly. The approach presented is one that has been experienced and with pain. There will be other variants to this approach.

The key message is that an ERP implementation is characterized by its complexity. There are lots of issues that need to be recognized and handled. Many have been identified in this book. No doubt there will be issues that have received scant or no attention. Every situation is unique. I hope that the content of this book has assisted the reader in alerting him to the detail of what is involved in an ERP implementation. The complexity of an ERP implementation is such that one cannot anticipate the unexpected, particularly when people are involved. The key tasks are to be informed about what might be, to be alert about what is happening and to pay attention to details, no matter how trivial they might appear. Activity is mandatory, though it must be sensible and co-ordinated within the grand scheme of things – the project plan.

An ERP implementation is about people. An information system only has value when people use it. Thus, people need to be involved in ensuring that it is used and, thus, has value. The opportunity to maximize this value is undermined by the problems that arise. Most technical issues can be fixed. People problems are more difficult to fix, if they can be fixed at all. The evidence for the latter is staff turnover, disputes and low levels of motivation. Politics or the interplay of self-interest can have a disturbing and negative impact. The project manager is a diplomat and a facilitator, is thick-skinned and resilient. The show will go on.

Selected reading

General

Baily, P., Farmer, D., Jessop, D. and Jones, D. (1998) *Purchasing Principles and Management*, 8th edn. Pitman Publishing, London

Camp, R.C. (1994) *Business Process Benchmarking: Finding and Implementing Best Practices*. ASQC Quality Press, Milwaukee

Senge, P. (1990) *The Fifth Discipline: The Art and Practice of the Learning Organisation*. Doubleday, New York

Project management and related

Remenyi, D. (1999) *Stop IT Project Failures: Through Risk Management*. Butterworth-Heinemann, Oxford

Remenyi, D., Money, A. and Sherwood-Smith, M. (2000) *The Effective Measurement and Management of IT Costs and Benefits*, 2nd edn. Butterworth-Heinemann, Oxford

Training

Minton, D. (1997) *Teaching Skills in Further and Adult Education*, 2nd edn. Macmillan, Basingstoke

Reece, I. and Walkers, S. (2000) *Teaching, Training and Learning: A Practical Guide*, 4th edn. Business Education Publishers, Sunderland

Reid, M.A. and Barrington, H. (1994) *Training Interventions: Managing Employee Development*, 4th edn. Institute of Personnel Development, London

Quality management

Atkinson, P.E. (1990) *Creating Culture Change: The Key To Successful Total Quality Management*. IFS Publications, Bedford

Dale, B.G. (1991) *Managing Policy*, 3rd edn. Blackwell, Oxford

Deming, W.E. (1982) *Out of the Crisis*. The M.I.T. Press, Cambridge, Massachusetts

Juran, J.M. (1992) *Juran on Quality by Design*. The Free Press, New York

Oakland, J. (1993) *Total Quality Management: The Route To Improving Performance*, 2nd edn. Butterworth-Heinemann, Oxford

Owen, M. (1993) *SPC and Business Improvement*. IFS Publications, Bedford

Business process reengineerng

Champy, J. (1995) *Reengineering Management: The Mandate for New Leadership*. HarperBusiness, New York

Obeng, E. and Crainer, S. (1994) *Making Re-engineering Happen*. Pitman Publishing, London

Organizational behaviour and culture

Handy, C. (1993) *Understanding Organisations*, 4th edn. Penguin, Harmondsworth

Morgan, G. (1997) *Images of Organisation*, 2nd edn. Sage Publications, Beverly Hills

Negotiation

Kennedy, G. (1998) *Kennedy on Negotiation*. Gower Publishing Ltd, Aldershot

Useful sources

A selection of enterprise application software vendors (as of 4th March 2002)

Name	Website
AremisSoft (Fourth Shift)	www.fseurope-com
BAAN (Invensys)	www.baan.com
Cognos	www.cognos.com
Epicor	www.epicor.com
Frontstep (Symix Systems Inc.)	www.frontstep.com
Geac (JBA)	www.geac.com
Glovia International	www.glovia.com
I2 Technologies	www.i2.com
IFS	www.ifsworld.com
Infor:swan	www.inforswan.co.uk
Intentia	www.intentia.com
JD Edwards	www.jdedwards.com
Made2Manage Systems	www.made2manage-com
Manugistics	www.manugistics.com
Mapics	www.mapics.co.uk
MAX International	www.max-international.com
McGuffie Brunton	www.mcguffie-co.uk
Navision	www.navision.com
Oracle	www.oracle-com
PeopleSoft	www.peoplesoft.com
QAD	www.qad.com
Ross Systems	www.rossinc.com
Sage (Tetra)	www.sageenterprisesolutions.com
Sanderson	www.sanderson.com

SAP	www.sap.com
Siebel	www.siebel.com
SSA GT	www.ssax.com
SSI	www.ssi-world.com
SSL	www.ssl.com

A selection of sites on erp and related issues

Benchmark Research Ltd	www.benchmark-research.co.uk
BPIC: the manufacturing planning resource	www.bpic.co.uk
CNET Networks Inc.	www.techrepublic.com
Gartner Inc.	www.gartner.com
IDC	www.idc.com
Manufacturing Systems	www.manufacturingsystems.com
The Workflow Management Coalition	www.wfmc.org

Acronyms and abbreviations

AP	Accounts Payable
APICS	American Production and Inventory Control Society
APS	Advanced Planning Systems
ASCII	American Standard Code for Information Interchange
ASP	Application Service Provider
B2B	Business To Business
B2C	Business To Customer
BI	Business Intelligence
BOM	Bills Of Materials
BOMP	Bill Of Material Processor
CAD	Computer Aided Design
CAM	Computer Aided Manufacturing
CD ROM	Compact Disk Read-Only Memory
CEO	Chief Executive Officer
CIM	Computer Integrated Manufacturing
COPICS	Communications Orientated Production Information and Control System
CRM	Customer Relationship Management
CRP	Capacity Requirements Planning
DOS	Disk Operating System
DSS	Decision Support Systems
EAI	Enterprise Application Integration
EDI	Electronic Data Interchange
EIS	Executive Information Systems
ERP	Enterprise Resource Planning

FTP	File Transfer Protocol
GRN	Goods Received Note
GUI	Graphical User Interface
HR	Human Resources
HTML	HyperText Mark-up Language
IDEF	Integration DEFinition
IS	Information Systems
IT	Information Technology
JIT	Just In Time
LAN	Local Area Network
MAP	Manufacturing Automation Protocol
MD	Managing Director
MRO	Maintenance, Repair and Overhaul
MRP	Material Requirements Planning
MRPII	Manufacturing Resource Planning
ODBC	Open Database Connectivity
OLAP	OnLine Analytical Processing
OPT	Optimized Production Technology
OSI	Open Standards Interconnection
PC	Personal Computer
PDM	Product Data Management
PO	Purchase Order
SCM	Supply Chain Management
SCP	Supply Chain Planning
SI	System Integrator
SLA	Service Level Agreement
SNA	Systems Network Architecture
SOP	Sales and Operations Planning
SQL	Structured Query Language
TCP/IP	Transmission Control Protocol/Internet Protocol
TOP	Technical and Office Protocols
TQM	Total Quality Management
UDDI	Universal, Description, Discovery and Integration
VAN	Value Added Network
VAR	Value Added Resellers
WAN	Wide Area Network
WAP	Wireless Application Protocol
WIP	Work In Progress
WWW	World Wide Web
XML	Extensible Mark-up Language
Y2K	Year 2000

References

1. Orlicky, J. (1975) *Material Requirements Planning*. McGraw-Hill, New York.
2. Wight, O.W. (1983) *The Executive's Guide to Successful MRPII*, 2nd edn. Oliver Wight Limited Publications, [location?]
3. Ralston, D. (1996) A brief history of manufacturing control systems – a personal view of where we went wrong. *Control (Institute of Operations Management)*, part 1, June, pp. 21–24; part 2, July/August, pp. 13–16; part 3, September, pp. 24–30; October, pp. 13–17.
4. Sadowski, R.P. (1984) History of computer use in manufacturing shows major need now is for integration. *Industrial Engineering*, March, pp. 34–42.
5. Boaden, R.J., Dale, B.G. (1986) What is computer-integrated manufacturing, *International Journal of Production Management*, 6 (3), 30–37.
6. Workflow Management Coalition (1995) *The Workflow Management Coalition Specification – Workflow Reference Model*, Document Number TC00–1003, Issue 1.1, www.wfmc.org
7. Codd, E.F., Codd, S.B., Salley, C.T. (1993) *Providing OLAP (OnLine Analytical Processing) to User-Analysts: An IT Mandate*, www.essbase.com
8. The OLAP Report, www.olapreport.com
9. Personal communication with Howard Dresner, Gartner Inc., 28th February 2002.
10. The Electronic Components Sector Group (1992) *'EDI'*. ISBN 0 7292 1038 3, National Economic Development Office, London.

11. Detailed accounts of the development of the Internet and WWW are to be found on the websites of the Internet Society (http://www.isoc.org) and R.H. Zakon (http://www.zakon.org). Another history is given by G. Gromov (http://www.netvalley.com)

12. Source: Internet Software Consortium (http://www.isc.org/)

13. Bickell, D. (1998) Hurdles to be tackled, *Computer Weekly*, 2 July, pp. 30–31.

14. Shaw, R., Davies, J. (2001) *Customer Relationship Management (CRM): overview*, Technical Overview: DPRO-90679, 11 October, Gartner Inc.

15. Gooding, C. (1995) A difficult sell to the sales staff, *Financial Times Review*, 1 November, p. 21.

16. McLean, H. (2001) Confused customers, *IT Consultant*, June, pp. 22–26.

17. Flood, G. (2000) Has CRM hit the heights, *Management Consulting*, October, pp. 15–19.

18. Bond, B., Genovese, Y., Miklovic, D., Wood, N., Zrimsek, B., Rayner, N. (2000) *ERP is Dead – Long Live ERPII*, Research Note SPA-12–0420, 4 October, Gartner Inc.

19. Genovese, Y., Bond, B., Zrimsek, B., Frey, N. (2001) *The Transition to ERPII: Meeting the Challenges*, Strategic Analysis Report: R-14–0612, 27 September, Gartner Inc.

20. Genovese, Y., Bond, B., Zrimsek, B., Frey, N. (2001) *The Transition to ERPII: Meeting the Challenges*, Strategic Analysis Report: R-14–0612, 27 September, Gartner Inc.

21. Evans, M., Bragg, S., Klevers, T. (1997) *OvumEvaluates: ERP for Manufacturers*. Ovum Ltd, London.

22. Meissner, G. (2000) *SAP: Inside the Secret Software Power*. McGraw-Hill, New York.

23. Davis, C. (2000) ASP model will combat the anarchy on firms' desktops, *Computer Weekly*, 22 June, p. 20.

24. Raviart, D. (2001) Time for a reality check, *Conspectus*, July, pp. 30–31.

25. Ashford, R.W., Dyson, R.G., Hodges, S.D. (1988) The capital-investment appraisal of new technology: problems, misconceptions and research directions, *Journal Operational Research Society 39* (7), 637–642.

26. Remenyi, D., Money, A., Sherwood-Smith, M. (2000) *The Effective Measurement and Management of IT Costs and Benefits*, 2nd edn. Butterworth-Heinemann, Oxford.

27. Remenyi, D., Money, A. Sherwood-Smith, M. (2000) *The Effective Measurement and Management of IT Costs and Benefits*, 2nd edn. Butterworth-Heinemann, Oxford.

28. Hammer, M. (1999) Re-engineering ERP, *Computer Weekly*, 28 October, p. 24.
29. Published by Findlay Publications, UK; www.mcsolutions.co.uk
30. Published by the PMP Group, UK; www.conspectus.com
31. Published by Reed Business Information, US; www.manufacturingsystems.com
32. Davis, M., Brown, D. (1999) *Markets and the Magic Quadrant Process*, 4 March, Gartner Inc.
33. Benchmark Research Ltd. (1994) *MRPII Implementation Satisfaction Survey*.
34. PA Consulting Group (2000) *Art and Science of Project Management: project culture: route to high performance*.
35. PA Consulting Group (2000) *Art and Science of Project Management: why do projects fail?*
36. Hammer, M. (1999) Re-engineering ERP, *Computer Weekly*, 28 October, p. 24.
37. Johnston, A.K. (1995) *A Hacker's Guide to Project Management*. Butterworth-Heinemann, Oxford.
38. Remenyi, D. (1999) *Stop IT project Failures: through risk management*, Butterworth-Heinemann, Oxford.
39. Gartner Inc. (1997) *Training: the underestimated ERP project requirement*, Research Note SPA-345–1337, 20 June, Gartner Inc.
40. Harwood, S.A. (1996) Re-thinking the business, *Business Change & Re-engineering*, 3 (3), 37–46.
41. Hammer, M. (1990) Reengineering work: don't automate, obliterate, *Harvard Business Review*, July–August, pp. 104–112.
42. Davenport, T.H., Short, J.E. (1990) The New Industrial Engineering: Information Technology and Business Process Redesign, *Sloan Management Review*, Summer, pp. 11–27.
43. Kilman, R.H., Saxton, M.J., Serpa, R. (1986) Issues in Understanding and changing culture, *California Management Review, XXVII* (2), 87–94.
44. Schein, E.H. (1984) Coming of a new awareness of organisational culture, *Sloan Management Review*, Winter, pp. 3–16.
45. Shrivastava, P. (1983) A typology of organisational learning systems, *Journal of Management Studies*, 20, 7–28.
46. Easterby-Smith, M. (1997) Disciplines of organisational learning: contributions and critiques, *Human Relations*, 50 (9), 1085–1113.
47. King, W.R. (2001) Strategies for creating a learning organisation, *Information Systems Management*, Winter, pp. 12–20.

Index